What's Your Life Worth?

ISBN 0-13-067165-7

9 780130 671653

92495

What's Your Life Worth?

Health Care Rationing...
Who Lives? Who Dies? Who Decides?

David Dranove

FT Prentice Hall
FINANCIAL TIMES

An Imprint of PEARSON EDUCATION
Upper Saddle River, NJ • New York • London • San Francisco • Toronto • Sydney
Tokyo • Singapore • Hong Kong • Cape Town • Madrid
Paris • Milan • Munich • Amsterdam

www.ft-ph.com

Library of Congress Cataloging-in-Publication Data

A catalog record for this book can be obtained from
the Library of Congress.

Editorial/production supervision: *Nick Radhuber*
Executive editor: *Tim Moore*
Editorial assistant: *Rick Winkler*
Marketing manager: *Alexis R. Heydt-Long*
Manufacturing buyer: *Maura Zaldivar*
Cover design director: *Jerry Votta*
Cover design: *Nina Scuderi*
Art director: *Gail Cocker-Bogusz*
Interior design: *Meg Van Arsdale*

 © 2003 Pearson Education, Inc.
Publishing as Financial Times Prentice Hall
Upper Saddle River, New Jersey 07458

Financial Times Prentice Hall books are widely used by corporations and
government agencies for training, marketing, and resale.

For information regarding corporate and government bulk discounts
please contact: Corporate and Government Sales (800) 382-3419 or
corpsales@pearsontechgroup.com

Company and product names mentioned herein are the trademarks
or registered trademarks of their respective owners.

Printed in the United States of America

10   9   8   7   6   5   4   3   2   1

ISBN 0-13-067165-7

Pearson Education LTD.
Pearson Education Australia PTY, Limited
Pearson Education Singapore, Pte. Ltd.
Pearson Education North Asia Ltd.
Pearson Education Canada, Ltd.
Pearson Educación de Mexico, S.A. de C.V.
Pearson Education—Japan
Pearson Education Malaysia, Pte. Ltd.

FINANCIAL TIMES PRENTICE HALL BOOKS

For more information, please go to www.ft-ph.com

Dr. Judith M. Bardwick
  Seeking the Calm in the Storm: Managing Chaos in Your Business Life
Gerald R. Baron
  Now Is Too Late: Survival in an Era of Instant News
Thomas L. Barton, William G. Shenkir, and Paul L. Walker
  *Making Enterprise Risk Management Pay Off: How Leading Companies
  Implement Risk Management*
Michael Basch
  *CustomerCulture: How FedEx and Other Great Companies Put
  the Customer First Every Day*
J. Stewart Black and Hal B. Gregersen
  Leading Strategic Change: Breaking Through the Brain Barrier
Deirdre Breakenridge
  Cyberbranding: Brand Building in the Digital Economy
William C. Byham, Audrey B. Smith, and Matthew J. Paese
  *Grow Your Own Leaders: How to Identify, Develop, and Retain
  Leadership Talent*
Jonathan Cagan and Craig M. Vogel
  *Creating Breakthrough Products: Innovation from Product Planning
  to Program Approval*
David M. Carter and Darren Rovell
  On the Ball: What You Can Learn About Business from Sports Leaders
Subir Chowdhury
  Organization 21C: Someday All Organizations Will Lead this Way
Subir Chowdhury
  The Talent Era: Achieving a High Return on Talent
Sherry Cooper
  Ride the Wave: Taking Control in a Turbulent Financial Age
James W. Cortada
  *21st Century Business: Managing and Working in the New
  Digital Economy*
James W. Cortada
  *Making the Information Society: Experience, Consequences,
  and Possibilities*
Aswath Damodaran
  *The Dark Side of Valuation: Valuing Old Tech, New Tech, and New
  Economy Companies*
Henry A. Davis and William W. Sihler
  Financial Turnarounds: Preserving Enterprise Value
Ross Dawson
  *Living Networks: Leading Your Company, Customers, and Partners
  in the Hyper-connected Economy*

Sarv Devaraj and Rajiv Kohli
The IT Payoff: Measuring the Business Value of Information Technology Investments

Harry Domash
Fire Your Stock Analyst! Analyzing Stocks on Your Own

David Dranove
What's Your Life Worth? Health Care Rationing...Who Lives? Who Dies? Who Decides?

Nicholas D. Evans
Business Agility: Strategies for Gaining Competitive Advantage through Mobile Business Solutions

Nicholas D. Evans
Business Innovation and Disruptive Technology: Harnessing the Power of Breakthrough Technology...for Competitive Advantage

Kenneth R. Ferris and Barbara S. Pécherot Petitt
Valuation: Avoiding the Winner's Curse

Oren Fuerst and Uri Geiger
From Concept to Wall Street

David Gladstone and Laura Gladstone
Venture Capital Handbook: An Entrepreneur's Guide to Raising Venture Capital, Revised and Updated

Marshall Goldsmith, Vijay Govindarajan, Beverly Kaye, and Albert A. Vicere
The Many Facets of Leadership

Robert B. Handfield, Ph.d, and Ernest L. Nichols
Supply Chain Redesign: Transforming Supply Chains into Integrated Value Systems

David R. Henderson
The Joy of Freedom: An Economist's Odyssey

Faisal Hoque
The Alignment Effect: How to Get Real Business Value Out of Technology

Harvey A. Hornstein
The Haves and the Have Nots: The Abuse of Power and Privilege in the Workplace...and How to Control It

Philip Jenks and Stephen Eckett, Editors
The Global-Investor Book of Investing Rules: Invaluable Advice from 150 Master Investors

Charles P. Jones
Mutual Funds: Your Money, Your Choice. Take Control Now and Build Wealth Wisely

Thomas Kern, Mary Cecelia Lacity, and Leslie P. Willcocks
Netsourcing: Renting Business Applications and Services Over a Network

Al Lieberman, with Patricia Esgate
The Entertainment Marketing Revolution: Bringing the Moguls, the Media, and the Magic to the World

Frederick C. Militello, Jr., and Michael D. Schwalberg
Leverage Competencies: What Financial Executives Need to Lead

Robin Miller
The Online Rules of Successful Companies: The Fool-Proof Guide to Building Profits

D. Quinn Mills
Buy, Lie, and Sell High: How Investors Lost Out on Enron and the Internet Bubble

Dale Neef
E-procurement: From Strategy to Implementation

John R. Nofsinger
Investment Blunders (of the Rich and Famous)...And What You Can Learn from Them

John R. Nofsinger
Investment Madness: How Psychology Affects Your Investing...And What to Do About It

Erica Orloff and Kathy Levinson, Ph.D.
The 60-Second Commute: A Guide to Your 24/7 Home Office Life

Tom Osenton
Customer Share Marketing: How the World's Great Marketers Unlock Profits from Customer Loyalty

Richard W. Paul and Linda Elder
Critical Thinking: Tools for Taking Charge of Your Professional and Personal Life

Matthew Serbin Pittinsky, Editor
The Wired Tower: Perspectives on the Impact of the Internet on Higher Education

W. Alan Randolph and Barry Z. Posner
Checkered Flag Projects: 10 Rules for Creating and Managing Projects that Win, Second Edition

Stephen P. Robbins
The Truth About Managing People...And Nothing but the Truth

Fernando Robles, Françoise Simon, and Jerry Haar
Winning Strategies for the New Latin Markets

Jeff Saperstein and Daniel Rouach
Creating Regional Wealth in the Innovation Economy: Models, Perspectives, and Best Practices

Ronald Snee and Roger Hoerl
Leading Six Sigma: A Step-by-Step Guide Based on Experience with GE and Other Six Sigma Companies

Eric G. Stephan and Wayne R. Pace
Powerful Leadership: How to Unleash the Potential in Others and Simplify Your Own Life

Jonathan Wight
Saving Adam Smith: A Tale of Wealth, Transformation, and Virtue

Yoram J. Wind and Vijay Mahajan, with Robert Gunther
Convergence Marketing: Strategies for Reaching the New Hybrid Consumer

About Prentice Hall Professional Technical Reference

With origins reaching back to the industry's first computer science publishing program in the 1960s, and formally launched as its own imprint in 1986, Prentice Hall Professional Technical Reference (PH PTR) has developed into the leading provider of technical books in the world today. Our editors now publish over 200 books annually, authored by leaders in the fields of computing, engineering, and business.

Our roots are firmly planted in the soil that gave rise to the technical revolution. Our bookshelf contains many of the industry's computing and engineering classics: Kernighan and Ritchie's *C Programming Language*, Nemeth's *UNIX System Adminstration Handbook*, Horstmann's *Core Java*, and Johnson's *High-Speed Digital Design*.

PH PTR acknowledges its auspicious beginnings while it looks to the future for inspiration. We continue to evolve and break new ground in publishing by providing today's professionals with tomorrow's solutions.

PRENTICE
HALL
PTR

CONTENTS

INTRODUCTION   xv

CHAPTER 1   IS IT NICE TO RATION?   1

PUTTING A PRICE ON YOUR LIFE   1
THE PRESSURE TO RATION   3
CUTTING TO THE CHASE   4
RATIONING DRUGS DOWN UNDER   8
THE NATIONAL INSTITUTE FOR CLINICAL
   EXCELLENCE (NICE)   10
   THE BETA-INTERFERON CONTROVERSY   15
   MEDICINE VERSUS ECONOMICS   17
ENDNOTES   19

CHAPTER 2   DEFENDING RATIONING IN PRINCIPLE   23

RATIONING AND TOY SHOPPING   25
ARE WE WASTING MONEY ON HEALTH CARE?   28
   MORAL HAZARD   29
   THE RAND STUDY   32
   DEMAND INDUCEMENT   33
   BAD BUYS IN HEALTH CARE   35
   THE WENNBERG VARIATIONS   37
DEFENDING RATIONING   38
ENDNOTES   39

CHAPTER 3   RATIONING AROUND THE WORLD   41

RATIONING IN GERMANY   44
  CONTROLLING DRUG COSTS IN GERMANY   46
  IF IT LOOKS LIKE RATIONING...   48
RATIONING IN CANADA   49
  THE CONSEQUENCES OF WAITING LISTS   50
  THE FUTURE OF RATIONING IN CANADA   51
RATIONING IN ENGLAND   52
RATIONING ELSEWHERE IN THE WORLD   54
ENDNOTES   55

CHAPTER 4   RATIONING IN THE U.S. HEALTH CARE MARKETPLACE   59

RATIONING THROUGH THE MARKET MECHANISM:
  THE UNINSURED IN THE UNITED STATES   60
ATTEMPTS TO PROVIDE UNIVERSAL COVERAGE   61
RATIONING AMONG INSURED AMERICANS   62
  GOVERNMENT-SPONSORED RATIONING IN THE
    UNITED STATES   64
  A BRIEF HISTORY OF MANAGED CARE   66
  MCO STRATEGIES FOR CONTAINING COSTS   67
WHITHER RATIONING IN AMERICA?   76
ENOUGH IS ENOUGH   77
ENDNOTES   78

CHAPTER 5   DOING COST-EFFECTIVENESS AND COST-BENEFIT RESEARCH   81

SOME BACKGROUND ON CEA   83
IS IT VALID TO USE CEA FOR HEALTH CARE?   83
DOING CEA/CBA   85
  MEASURING COSTS   87
  DISCOUNTING   90

Is CEA/CBA Research Valid? 92

CBA/CEA in Practice 93

Endnotes 96

CHAPTER 6 MEASURING THE QUALITY OF LIFE 97

Using Rating Scales to Measure Health
    States 98

Working with QALYs 99

Putting QALYs into Practice 102

    All QALYs Are Equal 102

    Measuring QALYs 103

    How Do Your QALY Scores Measure Up? 108

The Quality of Well-Being (QWB) Scale 110

Concerns about QALYs 111

    Discrimination and QALYs 112

    Limitations of QALY Surveys 112

Summing Up CEA/CBA Methods 113

What about the PSA Test? 114

Endnotes 115

CHAPTER 7 THE OREGON PLAN 117

Rationing in Oregon 117

The Story of Coby Howard 120

Toward a Rational Rationing Plan 121

    The Creation of the Oregon Health Plan 122

    The Oregon Plan and HMOs 123

    Creating the List 124

    The New List 126

    More Protests 128

The Performance of the Rationing Plan 131

Oregon Ten Years Later 133

Where Do We Draw the Line? 135

Endnotes 136

CHAPTER 8   WHAT IS YOUR LIFE WORTH?   139

WILLINGNESS TO PAY, HUMAN CAPITAL, AND
    INTRINSIC VALUE   140
PRICING LIFE IN THE REAL WORLD   142
THE COST-OF-ILLNESS (COI) APPROACH   143
USING SURVEYS TO PUT A PRICE
    ON GOOD HEALTH   145
    SOME WTP MEASURES   147
    WILLINGNESS TO PAY FOR LIFE   148
    HOW USEFUL ARE WTP MEASURES?   150
STATISTICAL VERSUS IDENTIFED LIVES   151
THE ECONOMIC APPROACH TO VALUING
    STATISTICAL LIVES   151
OTHER EVIDENCE ON THE VALUE OF LIFE   155
WHAT IS YOUR LIFE WORTH?   156
VALUE OF A QALY   157
RESPONDING TO MR. MORTIMER   158
THE BOTTOM LINE   159
ENDNOTES   160

CHAPTER 9   RISING COSTS AND RATIONAL
            RATIONING   163

THE HEALTH CARE BUDGET "CRISIS"   164
    THE DRAIN ON THE U.S. ECONOMY   165
TARGETING TECHNOLOGY   167
THE FALLACY OF COST CONTAINMENT   169
THE STEADY DRUMBEAT OF RATIONAL
    RATIONING   170
CAN PATIENTS BE RATIONAL?   172
WHO SHOULD RATION?   174
    RATIONAL RATIONING IN THE PUBLIC SECTOR   175
    RATIONAL RATIONING AND MANAGED CARE   177
    THE REAL OBSTACLES   179

Rational Rationing in the 21st Century   181
Endnotes   181

Index   183

INTRODUCTION

Y ou may not know it, but the people who pay for your health care have decided that enough is enough. They have placed a limit on how much they are willing to spend to save your life. In the United States, the keepers of the Medicare and Medicaid programs have capped spending growth, forcing providers to cut back on care. At the same time, U.S. employers are getting fed up with rising health insurance costs, and they are giving managed care organizations the go-ahead to cut back on prescription drug benefits and other services. Such restrictions are old news in the rest of the world, where government payers have been limiting access to costly medical technologies for over three decades.

This is rationing, plain and simple. Rationing is a dirty word in health care, but it is not necessarily a bad thing, provided the cost savings are large enough to justify any resulting harm. For the most part, rationing has been ad hoc, without careful weighing of the benefits and costs. But in the last few years, a few payers have taken baby steps toward rationalizing rationing—making sure that they get biggest bang out of their health care bucks.

This book is about the many ways in which health care is rationed, and the transition toward rational rationing. As Chapter 1 details, rational rationing has already been institutionalized by the British and Australian national health systems. The outcomes have been mixed. Government decision makers seem obligated to balance scientific principles with political considerations. The outcomes are not always pretty, and government health officials remain crippled by budget ceilings that force them to place an unrealistically low value on life.

Chapters 2 through 4 provide the theoretical justification for rationing health care and demonstrate the disconnect between theory and practice in Europe and the United States. At least for now, any careful weighing of lives and dollars seems to be mere happenstance. Chapters 5 and 6 describe rational rationing. Chapter 6 also explains how to numerically score different diseases to determine which are most worth curing. These methods appear to be relatively simple to implement. In fact, they were central to a rationing plan implemented a decade ago in the state of Oregon, as described in Chapter 7. But, as I show, appearances are deceiving. Proponents of rational rationing have yet to overcome numerous objections based on methodological, economic, ethical, and political grounds.

Even if supporters of rational rationing can overcome the myriad objections to it, their schemes will not fully succeed unless they can grapple with the most challenging obstacle of all. At some point, payers must decide where to draw the line and declare that one particular health care service is "worth it" whereas another, slightly less cost-effective service is not. To do this, payers will have to explicitly determine how much life is worth. Chapter 8 tackles this question head-on and even shows you how to compute the value of your own life.

One question remains: Who should implement rational rationing? Chapter 9 describes the global imperative to contain costs in the public and private sector. I argue that rational rationing is better left to the market, where individuals can decide for themselves how much their lives are worth. I conclude that if payers fully embrace rational rationing, they may no longer fear spending money to save lives.

1

Is It Nice to Ration?

Putting a Price on Your Life

The last time you were ill, you probably did not think about how much you would be willing to spend to get better. While you may not have thought about how much your health is worth, there is a chance that those who foot the medical bill have been doing the thinking for you. Some health care payers, including government payers in Australia and Great Britain, have been doing the unthinkable and placing a dollar value on life itself. The going rate for a year of life is about $50,000, give or take a few thousand. If your life is in the balance, but the cost of saving you exceeds $50,000, then your payer might decide that it is just not worth it. At least the British and Australians are being explicit about how much your life is worth, and they seem willing to increase spending if they think they are getting their money's worth. Government payers in Canada, Germany, and elsewhere have decided to draw a line on health care spending, regardless of the benefits. Employers in the United States, who foot the bill for most private health insurance, would like to do the same thing. They have apparently decided that it is just not worth spending more money to save lives, no matter how many lives are at stake.

We could dismiss these efforts to put a dollar value on life if the matter were some existential exercise. But the exercise has deadly real-world implications. Payers are using these numbers to ration health care services. If you ever become gravely ill, your payer might refuse to pay for your treatment on the grounds that the costs of treatment exceed the dollar value of the health care benefits. Your access to treatment—indeed, your life itself—may depend on how much your payer thinks your life is worth.

You may think that this idea is repugnant. How could a payer put dollars above life itself? In the classic 1974 book *Who Shall Live?* Victor Fuchs tackles this question head-on. He points out that societal resources are limited and that many other goals besides health care, "such as justice, beauty, and knowledge," also have a fair claim on resources.[1] We might argue that health is the most important goal of all. But does this imply that every person and every nation should spend whatever it takes to rid its people of disease, suffering, and unnecessary dying?

This is a laudable goal, but it is also an unaffordable goal. If we do all we can to limit disease, prevent suffering, and pro-long life, health care will claim the lion's share of our spend-ing. There will be little if anything left to spend on justice, beauty, food, the national defense, or whatever else we hold dear. As Fuchs observes, if we are to achieve all our goals, we must be willing to curtail spending on health care. This means we must ration health care.

According to economists, goods are rationed if, under the condition that goods are free, demand exceeds the supply. By this definition, virtually all goods and services are rationed. After all, few individuals have as much "stuff" as they would if everything were free. If clothing were free, cars were free, houses were free, we would all own more clothing, cars, and houses. But they are not free, so clothing, cars, and houses are rationed. Moreover, no one thinks that this rationing is unfair or unwarranted. It is simply a fact of life.

Health care is no exception to these principles. There is irrefutable evidence that we consume more health care services when someone else pays for them. We long ago abandoned any pretense that society could afford to allow patients unfettered access to free health care, so in the name of cost containment, we accede to access restrictions imposed by government regulators and managed care organizations (MCOs). But how much of their rationing should we accept?

THE PRESSURE TO RATION

Health care spending has increased steadily in the 30 years since Fuchs published *Who Shall Live?* and there is every reason to expect this trend to continue. Virtually every industrialized nation already spends at least 10 percent of its gross domestic product on health care; in the United States, one dollar out of every seven goes to health care. There are persistent and unyielding pressures for health care spending to increase in the years ahead. The population of the industrialized world continues to age. Perhaps more importantly, the march of medical science gives us the mixed blessing of powerful new treatments along with the bill to pay for them. If we do not want to drain additional resources away from other uses, we will have to ration health care spending even more. This view was perfectly expressed by a Canadian pediatrician questioning the wisdom of spending scarce resources on heart transplants. Without rationing, he felt, it would be impossible to assure basic health care services.[2]

As costs for new medical technologies such as transplants continue to mount, public and private sector payers have tried every means imaginable to hold the line on health care spending. Canada and England force patients to endure lengthy waits for costly services. France, Germany, and Japan limit physician and hospital fees. Australia refuses to pay for drugs that fail to provide health benefits that are commensurate with their costs. Health maintenance organizations (HMOs) in the United States pay bonuses to physicians who curtail utilization. These strategies contain the growth of health care costs but do not reverse the trend of cost increases.

Payers could continue the same old strategies for cost containment, but they are unlikely to be successful for long. There is only so much waste that can be cut out of the system. Patients can wait only so long for care. Providers will eventually refuse to accept further reductions in payments, or else the best and the brightest of our youth will be turned away from the medical profession. At the same time, medical science will continue to turn out new technologies that offer the promise of longer and better lives, but at a price. Either we will open the spigot and pour more money into health care, or we have to find new ways to ration.

In free markets, most goods are rationed by price. That is, sellers charge whatever price the market will bear, and goods are purchased by those who are willing to pay for them. Health insurance largely does away with rationing by price. In the past few decades, health services researchers have developed new tools for rationing, based on careful comparisons of the benefits and costs of medical care.[3] I call this *rational rationing*. Rational rationing offers a potential solution to rising health care costs, one that ensures that our health care dollars are spent wisely, and one that some payers have begun to implement.

CUTTING TO THE CHASE

The headline in the December 23, 2000, *London Daily Telegraph* read "MS Victims Angry as Drug Plan Is Shelved."[4] "Angry" was putting it mildly. Multiple sclerosis (MS) patients, their physicians, and advocacy groups were on the warpath. Medical experts had delayed the release of beta-interferon, a drug that could alleviate the symptoms of MS sufferers. To those affected, the medical experts responsible for the delay were nothing less than murderers.[5] The experts in question were physicians in England's National Institute for Clinical Excellence (NICE), an agency established in 1999 to assure that the best treatments are available to all patients. Andrew Dillon, the chief executive of NICE, stated that approval of beta-interferon would be delayed pending further economic modeling.[6] In the meantime, only those patients who could afford beta-interferon's £10,000 annual cost would receive it.

The beta-interferon controversy put health care rationing on the front page throughout England. But England is not the only nation that has institutionalized health care rationing in this way. In 1993, Australia set up new rules for pharmaceutical companies that wanted the national health system to pay for their new drugs. The drug makers were required to report economic data to the Pharmacy Benefits Advisory Committee (PBAC). PBAC rejected 40 percent of applications, many because of excessive costs. Among the drugs rejected by PBAC were Celebrex, for the treatment of arthritis, and Tolcapone, for the treatment of Parkinson's disease.

In Canada, rationing takes another form. Since the birth of the Canadian universal public health insurance system in 1971, the provinces have kept iron-fisted control over expenditures for facilities and equipment. The result has been long queues for a wide range of services. A 1993 study found that Canadian cancer patients had to wait three times longer for treatment than did their American counterparts.[7] A 1998 study documented excessive waits for cancer care, heart surgery, and neurological surgery, and a 2001 study found that the wait for various types of cancer surgery routinely exceeded five weeks.[8] The latter study found that one in every five patients had to wait more than two months for their surgery. By way of comparison, cancer experts consider waits of more than two weeks to be excessive.

Canadians put up with delays that seem almost too long to fathom, especially to Americans used to getting health care on demand. The wait for hip and knee replacements often exceeds six months. Cataract patients must wait up to a year for surgery. Things got so bad for flu sufferers in the winter of 2000 that patients occasionally had to wait days to receive treatment in hospital emergency rooms. According to one report, some patients spent their days in beds lining hospital corridors, and one patient died when his ambulance was diverted from the nearest hospital due to overcrowding.[9]

The most famous example of institutionalized rationing in the United States began in the state of Oregon in the early 1990s. The events that precipitated Oregon's rationing program started in 1987, when a boy covered by Oregon's Medicaid program (which provides insurance for the state's poor) died from leukemia. A bone marrow transplant might have saved his life, but Medicaid did not pay for such a costly procedure. This tragedy made headline news, and the state legislature quickly sought a better way to spend Medicaid dollars. (See Chapter 7 for more on this case.)

The legislature appointed a commission to develop a rationing scheme. In 1991, the commission released its report. Using methods that I describe in Chapter 6, the commission ranked medical interventions from those that offered the greatest benefit per dollar spent to those that provided little or no benefit per dollar. Interventions that ranked near the top of the list included antibiotic therapy for pneumonia and surgery for hernia repair. Interventions at the bottom included life support for extremely low birthweight babies and medical therapy for end-stage AIDS (this was before the introduction of the drug AZT).

Supporters of the rationing scheme proposed legislation that would cut off payment for those treatments that ranked at the bottom of the list in order to free up funds to pay for treatments in the middle and at the top. Opponents offered stinging criticism of the plan. The Children's Defense Fund questioned the fairness of rationing only poor people. Other groups claimed that the plan devalued the lives of the disabled. While many criticized the very notion of rationing, all ignored what the President of the Oregon Senate, John Kitzhaber (a former physician), accurately noted: that Oregon was already rationing medical care. The new program would merely bring it out into the open.[10]

Kitzhaber ignored the protests and pushed the state to implement the rationing plan. After considerable revision, the plan won federal approval, and in 1994, institutional rationing became a reality in Oregon. The state no longer pays for about 150 interventions (out of about 750 on the list), but it has expanded coverage to include dental care, preventive services, and organ transplants, and it has enrolled 100,000 previously uninsured residents. As the plan approaches its 10th anniversary, the residents of Oregon have learned to take the good with the bad, and on balance they seem to support the plan. Even so, no other state has seriously considered following Oregon's lead.

Rationing in the United States again took center stage during the 2001 congressional debate about patients' bill of rights legislation. Supporters of the legislation stated that they wanted to crack down on HMO cost-cutting tactics that interfered with good patient care. They solicited testimony from several families who suffered when their HMOs delayed or denied coverage. One HMO would not pay for psychological treatment of an anorexic teenager. The girl continued to suffer, and she took her own life at age 21. Another HMO refused to pay for physical therapy for a 4-year-old girl with spina bifida (a spinal disorder), even though six doctors said the therapy was medically necessary. Her parents spent months trying to persuade the HMO to change its mind. Eventually, the HMO agreed to pay for therapy, but only after her senator intervened in her behalf. There were many more stories like these, stories of patients who suffered because their HMOs rationed access to costly treatments.

HMOs have also systematized the rationing of prescription drugs. They have committees that create "formularies," which are lists of drugs that the HMOs will pay for. In the late 1990s many HMOs refused to pay for several new drugs, including Amerge (for the treatment of migraines) and Evista (for the treatment of osteoporosis). Patients in these HMOs had to pay for these drugs themselves (often at a cost of thousands of dollars annually) or do without.

As these examples show, governments and health insurance companies around the world systematically refuse to pay for some medical services, even when patients and their physicians believe those services may be valuable. Until recently, payers have relied on a combination of resource availability, politics, and medical research to decide what services they will cover, and what services they will require patients to pay for themselves. But they can do much better than this ad hoc approach to rationing.

Oregon's Medicaid program was the first to explicitly weigh the medical benefits and financial costs of different treatments. Though it sounds cold and calculated, such rational rationing has the potential to save lives *and* money. Some health services researchers want to go even further, by putting an explicit dollar value on life itself. Such a policy would have extraordinary implications. Imagine a payer refusing to pay for a drug that might extend the lives of some patients because the dollar cost of the drug exceeds the dollar value of the lives saved. This approach may seem brutally rational and borderline unethical, but it forms the foundation of two recent government-sponsored rationing plans: Australia's Pharmacy Benefits Scheme, and England's NICE program.

RATIONING DRUGS DOWN UNDER

Established in the 1940s, the Australian PBS provides universal coverage for all approved drugs.[11] Prior to 1993, approval was based on safety and efficacy. These are the main criteria used by drug regulators around the world, including the U.S. Food and Drug Administration. During the 1980s, drug expenditures in Australia grew at an annual rate of 6 percent, and the Australian government took action. In 1990, it announced that PBS approval would be based on safety, efficacy, and cost-effectiveness.

In 1993, the Australian government released new PBS guidelines that remain in effect today. Drug makers seeking PBS approval must submit economic evaluations to the Pharmaceutical Benefits Advisory Committee (PBAC), which reviews all new drugs and has also reviewed about one-third of the drugs that were on the PBS prior to 1993. Since the inception of the plan, PBAC has removed more than 60 drugs from the PBS. It has also delayed approval of many other drugs— often by as much as two years.

To win PBAC approval, drug makers must perform cost-effectiveness studies. Drug makers have responded to PBAC (and similar requirements by other regulators as well as MCOs) by establishing "pharmacoeconomics" departments. These departments perform cost-effectiveness studies, following the scientific principles spelled out later in this book. For PBAC submissions, these departments make head-to-head comparisons of their products against competitors. When a manufacturer can show that a new product is at least as cost-effective as the competition, the product stands a good chance of approval. Thus far, PBAC seems to be living up to its mandate of using cost-effectiveness analysis (CEA) in the drug approval process. Research shows that PBAC is significantly more likely to approve drugs with favorable cost-effectiveness ratios.[12]

This does not mean that PBS approval is now based solely on scientific analysis. In a few cases, drug makers and patients have successfully lobbied the government to bypass PBAC recommendations. For example, this occurred after PBAC rejected the breast cancer drug Herceptin for the third time. PBAC felt that the benefits of a few months' life extension did not justify the $600 (in U.S. dollars) weekly cost of the drug. This argument did not satisfy Herceptin's manufacturer, Roche, or the activist group Breast Cancer Network Australia. This group lobbied every member of the Australian Parliament, arguing that no one can put a price on life.[13] Under political pressure, the Australian government bypassed PBAC in 2002 and added Herceptin to the PBS.

PBAC also created controversy when it refused to approve Viagra. Viagra's maker, Pfizer, threatened to sue PBAC and then appealed PBAC's decision. PBAC held firm. Pfizer appealed again, presenting new evidence on Viagra's cost-effectiveness. Pfizer lost again. Pfizer appealed a third time, requesting that Viagra be approved for patients with a narrow range of conditions, including diabetes and spinal-cord injuries.[14] PBAC finally gave its approval for these limited uses.

PBAC's approval of Viagra has raised red flags among those concerned about budget priorities. Critics contend that Viagra use will soar, regardless of the PBAC limitations, and that the money spent on Viagra will be taken away from other, more valuable drugs. (They might have added that the money could have been put to good nonmedical uses as well.) Viagra is not the only budget-buster eventually approved by PBAC. Expenditures for cholesterol-lowering statin medications, arthritis drugs such as Celebrex, the smoking-cessation drug Zyban, and other therapeutic breakthroughs have taken their toll on the Australian drug budget. Drug expenditures are now climbing at a double-digit annual rate, twice the increase before PBAC was created. It is increasingly difficult for PBAC to balance the demand for valuable new drugs against its mandate to contain costs.

PBAC is caught in the middle of the classic debate about rationing. Opponents of the current Australian government, as well as critics of the pharmaceutical industry, claim that recently approved drugs are causing a "blowout" in the drug budget. They point out that in 2000, Celebrex and Zyban alone cost $180 million out of a total drug budget of $4 billion. Viagra was expected to add another $100 million in expenses. Critics mock this inordinate spending on "lifestyle" drugs and wonder if it will wreck the PBS. Yet patient groups are prepared to lobby to get every new drug on the PBS. Australian health minister Michael Wooldridge defends PBAC's "generosity," noting that decisions like the approval of Celebrex have been enthusiastically received, with patients actually stopping him on the street to express their gratitude.[15]

THE NATIONAL INSTITUTE FOR CLINICAL EXCELLENCE (NICE)

England's NICE is arguably the most famous (infamous?) rationing agency in the world. Ironically, NICE was formed to address widespread concerns about rationing that was already occurring. To understand why NICE was formed, it is necessary to first understand a little bit about the British National Health Service (NHS). Great Britain is divided into regional health authorities. Under the NHS, each health authority manages its own budget, and each must decide whether or not to pay for specific treatments, including prescription drugs. As a result, patients in one region may find that their authority will not pay for an expensive drug or surgery, even though other regional authorities cover it. This situation created what critics derisively called a "postcode lottery," so named because insurance coverage under the NHS depended where patients lived.

The postcode lottery was an unfortunate result of two conflicting trends. First, rapidly evolving technology made it possible to treat conditions such as breast cancer, dementia, and MS, but only at a very high cost. Second, economic growth across England was uneven. Some health authorities, such as Somerset, had ample budgets, but others, such as Avon, did not. Patients lucky enough to live in Somerset could count on coverage for Taxol to treat breast cancer and beta-interferon to treat MS. But Avon residents were not so lucky. Their health authority could earmark only £120,000 annually for beta-interferon, enough to treat just 12 patients. Hundreds of others had to go without.

By the mid-1990s, there was a growing consensus in Britain that the NHS needed to put an end to the postcode lottery. Newspapers put pressure on the NHS by profiling patients denied access to drugs, even though neighbors living across the street (but in a different health region) had coverage. In the summer of 1998, when Viagra was poised to hit the market, several newspapers had a field day speculating about possible "sex by postcode,"[16] while in 1999, an MS sufferer successfully sued the North Derbyshire Health Authority to obtain coverage for beta-interferon. Physicians, patients, and many politicians all called on the NHS to increase funding to cash-starved regional authorities.

On April 1, 1999, the NHS acted to end the postcode lottery. Following Australia's lead in institutionalizing cost-effectiveness as a decision-making tool, the NHS established NICE. Nominally, NICE's role is "to provide patients, health professionals and the public with authoritative, robust and reliable guidance on 'best practice.'[17] The Secretary of State for Health selects the topics for "guidances," based on their likely impact on the NHS. The current Secretary, Frank Dobson, has claimed that NICE would put an end to postcode rationing[18] and instead would make sure that the availability of drugs and other technologies would be based on evidence of cost-effectiveness.

This was hardly the first time that a health care payer would rely on clinical evidence. Throughout the world, payers have for years refused to cover services for which there was no evidence of efficacy (that is, no evidence that the service did any good). This is a practice that all medical providers have come to accept. But Dobson went further. NICE would not just consider efficacy. NICE also intended to consider efficiency. Even if a service was efficacious, NICE might not approve it. That depended on how much it cost. Like Australia's PBS, NICE would explicitly trade off benefits and costs.

If anyone doubted NICE's determination to weigh costs as well as benefits, such doubts were eliminated after NICE issued its first guidance. In October 1999, NICE published its guidance on the prescription of Relenza, an antiviral drug made by British pharmaceutical giant Glaxo. There is almost no doubt that Relenza is efficacious in reducing flu symptoms; it is routinely covered by even the stingiest of HMOs in the United States. But the NICE guidance on Relenza cited the high cost of the drug (at least £9.9 million annually, out of a total NHS budget of £65 billion) and the minimal health benefit (one day reduction in symptoms for some patients). In light of this evidence, NICE advised against the prescription of Relenza during the 1999–2000 influenza season. NICE added that it expected to examine additional data and might revise the guidance.

The NHS went along with the Relenza guidance. For the first time in England, the NHS cited high costs to refuse to pay for a medically efficacious treatment. Needless to say, this angered providers and patients. It also angered pharmaceutical companies. Drug makers had hoped that NICE would prevent the postcode lottery by assuring wider access to drugs.

Instead, NICE appeared to be limiting access. Tom McKillop, the head of the British Pharma trade group, complained to Prime Minister Tony Blair that the ruling on Relenza had fulfilled their companies' worst fears about NICE, namely, that NICE was a smoke screen for rationing of health services.[19] McKillop also wrote an editorial in the *London Daily Telegraph* whose title, "Postcard Prescribing Is Better Than No Prescribing," succinctly summed up its message.[20] In the meantime, Glaxo CEO Richard Sykes sent a letter to Secretary Dobson in which he threatened to move his company out of the United Kingdom. Other pharmaceutical firms made similar threats.

Having issued just one guidance, NICE had already learned that nothing it would ever do would be entirely free of political considerations. NICE reacted by treading with caution. First, it promised to assess additional evidence on the cost-effectiveness of Relenza. Then, it waited five months before issuing its second guidance. It chose a far less controversial procedure— the removal of wisdom teeth. By April 2000, however, the storm over Relenza had died down. In the meantime, NICE had performed detailed studies of several drugs and medical services and began offering a series of new guidances. In April 2000, NICE recommended against the use of several costly types of hip prostheses. To justify this action, NICE cited the lack of good cost-effectiveness data.[21] In May 2000, NICE recommended increased use of coronary artery stents, instead of coronary artery bypass surgery, to open blockages in the cardiac circulatory system.

That same month, NICE approved the use of a class of drugs called taxanes for the treatment of ovarian cancer. In June, NICE approved the same drugs for the treatment of breast cancer. These were crucial rulings because the NHS had refused to pay for these costly new drugs, pending the NICE guidelines. Moreover, an unfavorable ruling might have created a potent political alliance between women's health groups and the pharmaceutical industry. For the time being, NICE had avoided further controversy.

Perhaps because of the favorable ruling, potential critics of NICE seemed to overlook a remarkable paragraph that appears in the ovarian cancer guidance. Buried in a section titled "Evidence," NICE reported that research on the cost-effectiveness of taxanes suggested a *cost per life-year gained* of £6,000 to £8,000 per patient.[22] For the first time, NICE explicitly weighed money against lives and publicly stated its findings. The message that was lost in the fine print was a crucial one: NICE would recommend that the NHS spend the money to save lives, but only if the price was right. Moreover, NICE felt that £8,000 per year of life was cheap enough. This raised an interesting question. What if the cost had been £80,000 per year of life? Would NICE and the NHS have concluded that the price was too high? Would they have refused to pay for treatment because they did not believe a year of life was worth that much?

Over the next year, NICE guidances would provide some answers. Most guidances now report specific trade-offs between money and lives. NICE supports the use of gemcitabine for the treatment of pancreatic cancer, based on a cost per life-year of £7,200 to £18,700. It recommends against the use of implantable heart defibrillators, which cost upwards of £30,000 per life-year saved. In its revised Relenza guidance, issued in late 2000, NICE supports the drug's use among at-risk adults, citing a cost per year of life of £9,300 to £31,500, but recommends against its use among all adults, citing a cost per life-year of £38,000. (Actually, NICE refers to the costs per quality-adjusted life-years (QALY), which is not quite the same thing as a regular year. I will have a lot more to say about QALYs in Chapter 6.) In a guidance restricting the use of laparoscopic surgery to only certain types of hernia repair, NICE cites a cost per life-year of £50,000. Apparently, NICE believes that it may be worth spending £30,000 for a year of life but balks when the price approaches £40,000. As far as NICE is concerned, a year of life must be worth between £30,000 and £40,000. (One study estimates that Austrailia's PBAC uses an implicit threshold of about $50,000 [in U.S. dollars] per life-year.[23])

Thus far, NICE has issued more than 50 guidances. Almost all of them explicitly weigh costs and benefits, and they base recommendations on the estimated cost per year of life. But none have received more attention or criticism than NICE's guidance on beta-interferon.

THE BETA-INTERFERON CONTROVERSY

By late June 2000, NICE had issued six guidances, half of which placed substantial restrictions on access to care. Even so, the public reaction to these restrictions was mild in comparison to the reaction to a ruling that NICE did not issue. On June 21, 2000, word leaked out that NICE would recommend against the use of beta-interferon for the treatment of MS.

MS is a disease of the central nervous system. MS patients suffer many symptoms, including double vision, fatigue, and poor coordination. These symptoms may come and go in some MS patients, but the disease usually progresses, and the symptoms cease going into remission. When the injectable drug beta-interferon was first proposed as a treatment for MS, research suggested that it was efficacious in reducing the frequency and intensity of symptoms in some patients. The British Association of Neurologists stated that the evidence of the drug's efficacy was unequivocal. Based on such evidence, regulators approved the drug for sale in England in 1995.

Even so, all but nine (out of 100) regional health authorities balked at the cost of the drug, with the result that only 2 percent of MS sufferers in the UK took the drug, versus 12 to 16 percent elsewhere in Europe.[24] MS patients had hoped that NICE would support the use of beta-interferon, opening the way for more generous coverage and wider access. The leaked ruling from NICE disappointed and angered MS patients, family members, providers, and rival politicians. Newspapers were filled with personal testimonials about the benefits of beta-interferon. "I can sit up in bed," said one patient,[25] while another told of how the drug allowed her to read to her children.[26] The Sunday *London Daily Telegraph* featured an article written by an MS patient, titled "The Hope Interferon Gives Me."[27] The author was "shocked and angered" by NICE's claim that beta interferon was not cost-effective and described NICE as "viciously cruel."

NICE Chairman Michael Rawlins did not dispute any of the arguments put forth by MS supporters. Confirming the content of the unreleased report, he stated that NICE did not approve beta-interferon because the cost outweighed the benefits.[28] In fact, one research study suggested that the cost per QALY approached £1 million, well above the threshold that had been used in other guidances. This rational assessment did little to quell the anger of MS supporters. Activists organized letter-writing campaigns across England. Newspapers around the country continued to run articles about the controversy. Members of Parliament put political pressure on the NHS to ignore NICE and pay for beta-interferon. In the meantime, a firm that manufactured the drug released a study showing that the cost per QALY was less than £40,000, right around the NICE threshold.

The protests paid off. By the end of July 2000, NICE had agreed to postpone issuing its report on beta-interferon until September. September came and went, but no report was forthcoming. In December, NICE announced that it would not release its report until 2001; one month later, NICE indicated that the report would be delayed by another six months. By August 2001, the report had been put off yet again. In the meantime, most regional authorities still refused to pay for the drug. NICE officials were accused of "breathtaking bungling" and branded murderers.[29] NICE finally released its beta-interferon guidance in February 2002. Striking a middle ground, NICE allowed current users to continue to receive the drug but recommended against paying for the drug for new patients.

While it dragged its feet on beta-interferon, NICE issued many other guidances. Whereas half the guidances issued prior to June 2000 placed moderate to severe restrictions on access, virtually all of the guidances issued in the wake of the beta-interferon fiasco were lenient (though some narrowed the range of candidate patients on the basis of clinical conditions). It approved Ritalin for children with attention deficit disorder and acetylcholinesterase inhibitors for treating Alzheimer's disease. The revised Relenza guidance reversed the previous restrictions on its use.

Was the string of favorable guidances a coincidence? Perhaps all of the therapies considered by NICE were truly cost-effective. But it is also possible that NICE withheld unfavorable guidances until the controversy died down. In fact, when news leaked out in May 2001 that NICE planned to recommend against paying for a drug treatment for non-Hodgkin's lymphoma, some critics contended that NICE intended to withhold the announcement until after the June election for prime minister. Yet after the election, NICE continued to issue mostly favorable guidances. It approved nicotine replacement therapy for smokers who wished to quit, and guidance on obesity okayed the prescription of Meridia.

Judging from the public's reaction to negative guidances, one wonders why NICE does not approve everything. In June 2002, NICE restricted funding for Visudyne, an intravenous drug that treats macular degeneration, the leading cause of blindness in the elderly. The drug is routinely available in Europe, the United States, and Canada. But citing a cost per QALY of £80,000, NICE effectively restricted the use of Visudyne to one eye, provided the patient had already lost sight in the other. As with the proposed restriction on beta-interferon, the public has reacted hostilely, to say the least. One leading newspaper ran the headline "You Must Go Blind in One Eye Before NHS Will Treat You."[30] Another ran "Eye Treatment Proposals Are Scandalous."[31] Still another claimed, "Ruling Will Let Thousands Go Blind."[32] Thus far, NICE has refused to revisit its ruling, but political pressure is mounting.

MEDICINE VERSUS ECONOMICS

In making cost-benefit trade-offs explicit, NICE was sure to draw fire from the medical community. From the first day of medical school, fledgling physicians are taught to do whatever is possible to improve the health of their patients. Physicians are restrained only by the dictum "Do no harm." Naturally, the thought that cost might stand in the way of a potentially valuable treatment is anathema to physicians.

In contrast, economists have long counseled in favor of weighing medical benefits against costs. Academic economists and even a few medical researchers have been publishing cost-effectiveness studies for more than three decades. These studies have questioned the widespread use of interventions such as bypass surgery, liver transplants, and even the prescription of antibiotics for sore-throat sufferers. In the past few years, rising medical costs, especially the costs of prescription drugs, have forced more and more decision makers in the health care community to give credence to the economists' viewpoint. In many countries, including England and Canada, patients have come to accept a certain degree of rationing. In the United States, patients have implicitly given their approval for rationing as well. Patients may object when they are the personal victims of rationing by HMOs. But, when given the choice, many Americans balk at paying for more expensive forms of health insurance in which rationing is all but nonexistent.

As the medical research community rolls out new technologies at a record pace, and as aging baby boomers demand that their medical systems pay for them, health care costs will continue to rise. At some point, all payers will face the same problem as the one confronting the British NHS: In a world of limited resources, it may be necessary to curtail health care purchases. When this happens, rationing will take center stage throughout the world.

This is not to say that rationing is relatively new to health care. In a lecture titled "The Morality of Efficiency in Health Care," British economist Anthony Culyer observed that rationing was an everyday occurrence long before payers got involved.[33] Culyer recalled the example of a British physician who was listening to a patient with psychological problems describe his personal anguish. The story continued, "Suddenly, the phone rings—a 55-year-old lecturer with a history of chest pains has collapsed in a lecture room. [The physician] excuses himself from the patient before him, being the only physician on duty, to attend to the patient outside." This physician has rationed his time, deciding that "the cost of temporarily neglecting the one is justified by the immediate need of the other." Culyer told the story of another physician whose patient had requested the latest and most expensive nonsteroidal anti-inflammatory drug (NSAID). The physician recommended an effective but much cheaper NSAID. The patient was outraged. She felt that her physician was withholding a valuable treatment—that is, she was being rationed—and switched physicians.

Few people notice when rationing is the result of decisions made by individual physicians. There are certainly no newspaper headlines, and there is no handwringing by politicians. But institutional rationing is another story. Rationing by HMOs leads to emotionally charged hearings and congressional reforms. Britain's NICE, which has taken a scientific approach to rationing, has been met with skepticism and scorn. No organization wants the kind of scathing publicity brought about when it rations health care. It stands to reason that these organizations—government agencies and HMOs alike—have some overwhelming reason for wanting to ration.

Institutional rationing replaces the decisions of doctors and patients with third-party command and control. This makes sense only if unfettered medical decision making, free of institutional interference, is fraught with inefficiencies and mistakes. Chapter 2 documents these inefficiencies and mistakes. Their magnitude is staggering. The waste of unfettered medical decision making amounts to several hundred billion dollars annually. Medical mistakes costs thousands of lives. This financial and human toll forms the backbone of the argument in favor of rationing.

ENDNOTES

1. V. Fuchs, 1974, *Who Shall Live?* New York: Basic Books.

2. P. Metcalf, 1993, "Is Heart Transplantation a Wise Use of Scarce Health Care Dollars?" *Canadian Medical Association Journal* 149(12): 1829–30.

3. Health services researchers are mainly physicians and social scientists who study ways to improve the performance of health care systems.

4. C. Hall, "MS Victims Angry as Drug Plan Is Shelved," *London Daily Telegraph* 23 December 2000, p. 4.

5. R. Yeo, "MS Group Is Angry at Drug Decision Today," *UK Newsgroup Regional Press—This Is Bradford.*

6. Hall, ibid.

7. Reported in M. Walker, 1999, "The Americas: Canadians with Medical Needs Follow Their Doctors South," *Wall Street Journal* 15 March 1999, p. A15.

8. "Heresy in Canada," *Wall Street Journal* 29 November 1999, p. A14. P. Yelaha, 2001, "Cancer Surgery Wait Called Shocking," *Toronto Star* 21 August 2001, p. 1.

9. J. Beltrame, "To Ease Crisis in Health Care, Canadians Eye Private Sector," *Wall Street Journal* 20 April 2000, p. A19.

10. M. Abramowitz, 1992, "Oregon Plan Would Ration Health Care, Cover Every Resident," *Washington Post* 14 June 1992, p. B4.

11. For more information, see J. Hall, 1999, "Incremental Change in the Australian Health Care System," *Health Affairs* 18(3): 95–110.

12. D. Birkett, A. Mitchell, and P. McManus, 2001, "A Cost-Effectiveness Approach to Drug Subsidy and Pricing in Australia," *Health Affairs* 20(3): 104–14.

13. See M. King, 2001, "Up to 900 Women Gain Help in High-Cost Battle with Tumours," *The Advertiser* 19 October 2002, p. 22.

14. "Viagra Listing Raises Issue of Cost Blowout," *Canberra Times* 20 January 2002, p. 22.

15. M. Blenkin, 2001, "Fed: Wooldridge Says Government Aims to Stop Drug Wastage," *AAP Newsfeed* 3 June 2001.

16. J. Laurance, "Viagra on NHS May Cost Pounds 1Bn," *The Independent* 8 July 1998, p. 9. The British NHS took the regional authorities off the hook for Viagra by issuing a nationwide ban on coverage.

17. NICE web site: *www.nice.org.uk/cat.asp?c=43.*

18. NICE web site: *www.nice.org.uk/cat.asp?a=28.*

19. A. Clark, "Sick of Being Patient," *London Daily Telegraph* 9 October 1999, p. 31.

20. *London Daily Telegraph*, 11 October 1999, p. 24.

21. NICE, "Guidance on the Selection of Prostheses for Primary Total Hip Replacement," April 2000.

22. NICE, "Guidance on the Use of Taxanes for Ovarian Cancer," May 2000.

23. Hall, ibid.

24. Statistics cited in T. Womersley, G. Jones, and D. Demetriou, "MS Sufferers Condemn NHS Curb on Drug Treatment," *London Daily Telegraph* 22 June 2000, p. 1.

25. Quoted in J. Duddy, 2000, "MS Patients Refute Claims," *Plymouth Evening Herald* 23 June 2000, p. 13.

26. Quoted in Womersley et al., ibid.

27. A. Palmer, "The Hope Interferon Gives Me," *London Sunday Telegraph* 25 June 2000, p.34.

28. "NICE Review After Further Leak," *Chemist and Druggist* 1 July 2000, p. 6.

29. Hall, ibid.

30. J. Chapman and J. Hope, 2002, *London Daily Mail*, 13 June 2002, p. 2.

31. J. Hodby, 2002, *Leicester Mercury* 14 June 2002, p. 12.

32. L. Burkin, 2002, *London Evening Standard* 13 June 2002, p. 25.

33. A. Culyer, 1993, "The Morality of Efficiency in Health Care," in A. King, T. Hyclak, R. Thornton, and S. McMahon, eds., *North American Health Care Policy in the 1990s,* New York: John Wiley & Sons Limited. Reproduced with permission.

CHAPTER

2 DEFENDING RATIONING IN PRINCIPLE

It is not easy to defend rationing of any good or service. Rationing evokes images of bread lines in the old Soviet Union and interminably long waits for gasoline in the United States during the 1972 Arab oil embargo. Rationing in health care has even worse connotations. When an African dies from AIDS because he cannot afford to pay for drugs, and the drugmaker refuses to provide them for free, he has been rationed. When an uninsured woman in the United States is refused lifesaving cardiac surgery for financial reasons, she too has been rationed. These dramatic depictions of rationing are easy to conjure up, but hard to justify.

Rationing can be far more mundane. In fact, we have all rationed and we have all been rationed. And we sometimes think that rationing is a good thing, or at worst a necessary evil. Here is one of countless examples of rationing. Say you are having a pizza party and you order enough to serve 12 people. Unfortunately, some of your friends invite some of their friends, and you end up with 20 guests. To make sure that everybody gets some pizza, you ask your guests to limit themselves to two slices each. You are rationing.

The pizza parlor can make only a limited number of pizzas. It cannot offer its pizza to anyone who wants some, so it too has to ration. It probably rations by charging for each pizza. Economists say that the pizza parlor *rations by price*. Through price rationing, it makes pizzas only for people who are willing to pay for them. Virtually all markets feature rationing by price. Rationing by price is a good way to make sure that products like pizza go to the consumers who value them the most. Rationing by price also assures that if consumers show an increased desire to pay for a good, sellers will increase production. This is one of the virtues of price rationing in the marketplace. It makes sure that sellers produce the goods and services that consumers value the most.

Price rationing is so effective in the pizza market that one would be hard-pressed to come up with a justification for the government to step in and implement its own scheme for rationing pizza. One could imagine the government creating a Regional Institute for Pizza Excellence (RIPE). RIPE could commission research to study the benefits and costs of various pizzas and then ban purchases of pizzas that fail to deliver enough QAPYs (Quality Adjusted Pizza Yummies) per dollar. This would be ludicrous. We do not need RIPE to tell us what kind of pizza to purchase. Such meddling would be unthinkable.

Some of us might sooner tolerate meddling in pizza markets than in health care markets. After all, if the government messed up the pizza market, it would hardly be the end of the world. But if the government, or an HMO for that matter, messed up the health care market, it might literally be the end of the world for some people. So, if institutional rationing of pizza is unheard-of, why would anyone think of allowing a government agency, or an HMO, to tell us what health care services we can and cannot buy?

If we follow the pizza analogy, the case for third-party involvement in health care rationing seems dead on arrival. Most consumers highly value their health, so the market ought to ensure an ample supply of health care services. In fact, spending in unregulated health care markets generally exceeds spending in regulated markets. Therein lies the problem. Many people believe that free-market health care spending is excessive, and they advance arguments in favor of institutional rationing. Bear in mind that their arguments defend rationing *in theory*. As subsequent chapters will show, however, there is a big difference between theory and practice.

RATIONING AND TOY SHOPPING

Before I defend the theory of rationing, it will be helpful to discuss rationing of another product that seemingly has nothing to do with health care, or pizza for that matter. This section describes parental rationing of new toys.

If you are a parent of a young child, and your experiences are anything like mine, then you undoubtedly have mixed feelings about taking your child to the toy store. There is the delight you and your child share when you pick out a new plaything. But there is always the dreaded moment when your child asks for something that you have no intention of buying. No matter how much your child nags you, your parental duty to select your children's toys comes first. No one would blame you for turning down an unreasonable request. It is okay to ration toy purchases.

Let us make this example a bit more concrete. Suppose that you take your son to the toy store. It is a special outing, as you are going to pick out a birthday present for your daughter. Of course, you also plan to buy something for your son, just to keep him quiet! You have budgeted $20 for the outing. Unfortunately, before you have a chance to pick out your daughter's present, your son is begging for a construction set that costs $19. Normally, you might purchase such an extravagance, but in this case, you have to turn him down. The construction set could make your son a bit happier, but your daughter might be devastated if all she received for her birthday was a little toy that cost just $1.

You have good reason to ration your son. He has failed to see the "greater good" for the family that can be done by spending the $20 wisely. Instead, he is thinking only of his own wants, and not those of his sister. By considering the alternative uses for your cash, you are making sure that you get the most for your family's money. I call this the "biggest bang for the buck" (BBB) rationing defense.

The BBB defense applies whenever one person is doing the shopping but someone else is footing the bill. The shopper might think only of his or her own needs. But the person paying the bill has other needs to worry about. There are many familiar examples of the BBB defense. Employers limit employee entertainment expenses to avoid spending so much on drinks and food that there is not enough left to run the business. Homeowners preapprove their interior decorators' purchases to avoid spending so much on the dining table that there is no money left to put food on it.

The BBB defense applies to health care as well. Doctors do the "shopping" (that is, they select the treatments), but payers foot the bill. Some doctors might recommend costly services that provide only minimal benefits. Patients will probably consent, knowing that someone else is paying. Payers want to be sure that the available resources serve the patients with the greatest needs. To do this, they might require physicians to obtain permission before they can render costly treatments, or in some other way limit the doctors' ability to provide care. In this way, payers assure that patients collectively get the biggest bang for their health care bucks.

There is another kind of rationing that tries to cut down on the total health care budget. To better understand this kind of rationing, it is helpful to return to the toy store. Suppose that you have successfully persuaded your son to accept a small toy and have even had time to pick out your daughter's present. You are on your way to the checkout line when disaster strikes. Your little boy spies a stuffed animal and begs you to buy it. You recall that the last time you bought your son a stuffed animal, he threw it under the bed, where it has been gathering dust ever since. You refuse to buy another one.

Once again, you have every reason to ration your son. You know a worthless purchase when you see one, and no amount of complaining can get you to waste your money. I call this the "waste of money" (WOM) rationing defense. As with the BBB defense, the WOM defense arises when the person doing the shopping does not foot the bill. The difference is that under the BBB defense, the shopper does a poor job of choosing among alternative ways to spend money. Under the WOM defense, the shopper probably shouldn't be spending money at all.

Health care payers often use the WOM defense to justify intervening in the medical process. They claim that physicians ignore costs and often provide expensive treatments that offer no benefits. Patients do not know any better, and besides, they do not care about the cost. The result is that everyone's health care costs increase without any benefit to patients. Like BBB rationing, WOM rationing can involve limits on the supply of services, or requirements that providers obtain approval for care.

BBB and WOM rationing smack of paternalism. It is okay for a parent to be paternalistic toward a child—that is where the term comes from. When it comes to rationing in health care, however, physicians and patients play the child's role, and such paternalism is distinctly unwelcome. Who can blame physicians for getting angry about having to obtain permission to treat their patients? What patient wants to wait three months to obtain an MRI, or beg an insurer to cover the costs of surgery? Our instinctive hostility to paternalism is a major obstacle to health care rationing. Any defense of rationing must overcome this obstacle by making the case that we are all better off when we allow payers to look over our shoulders and, occasionally, to say no to our demands for medical care.

In the remainder of this chapter, I advance two arguments to justify rationing. First, we are wasting tremendous amounts of money on health care (the WOM defense). Second, within a limited health care budget, we can do a better job of deciding what health care services we should and should not receive (the BBB defense). These arguments are necessary, but not sufficient, to justify rationing. After all, the fact that we as individuals do not always make the best decisions does not, by itself, justify someone else making those decisions for us. But without these arguments, there is no case at all to be made for rationing.

ARE WE WASTING MONEY
ON HEALTH CARE?

Back in the 1960s, health care in the United States accounted for 5 percent of the gross domestic product (GDP). Now it accounts for nearly $1 of every $7 spent, or about $5,000 per capita. Health care is big business outside the United States as well. In most nations that have a government-sponsored health insurance program, health care is the largest public sector program, accounting for as much as half of government spending. Many policymakers continue to believe that much of this spending is wasteful, and they use this argument to justify cutbacks in health care programs.

It is one thing to justify rationing with claims that we are wasting money on health care. It is quite another thing to prove it. Ever increasing costs seem like prima facie evidence of waste. Yet similarly prolonged growth in any other sector of the economy, accompanied by steady improvements in quality, would probably be a source of national pride.[1] It would be unheard-of to complain, "Spending on consumer electronics is out of control" or to ask, "How can we rein in the motion picture industry?" Why then, do we voice these complaints about health care?

One source of contention in the U.S. health care system is the high administrative expenditures for marketing, running insurance companies, bill collection, and other activities that do not directly improve patient care. But high administrative expenses cannot explain why the United States spends 50 percent more than any other nation on health care, or why costs have risen steadily for more than 40 years. Moreover, although administrative expenses are much lower in other nations, the concern about rising costs is global. Clearly, any efforts to contain health care costs must reign in excessive medical expenditures, not just administrative costs.

This statement presumes, of course, that medical expenditures are excessive. Many people believe that our health is our most important possession and that we should spend as much as we can to protect and improve it. One might therefore argue that medical expenditures can never be excessive. This could be a persuasive argument if health care services were consistently effective. But a lot of health care spending is for services that provide little to no value. By one account, 70 percent of medical treatment is provided without a firm scientific basis, and much of this has questionable value.[2] If true, then our health care expenditures are wildly excessive, and rationing is very much in order.

MORAL HAZARD

Throughout the developed world, physicians control the majority of medical expenditures. If patients receive nearly worthless treatments, it is because physicians order them. Why would physicians order worthless services? Perhaps they want to satisfy sick patients who hope their doctors will "do something" to cure them. In that case, the services may provide some psychological benefit. But economists offer other explanations for wasteful spending based on the unusual financial incentives facing patients and providers alike.

The economists' first argument goes like this: When consumers go shopping for most goods and services, they pay for everything themselves. As a result, consumers are careful shoppers. But when patients obtain health care services, someone else—the insurance company—usually pays. As a result, patients are not such good shoppers. They care only that the health care services might provide a modicum of benefit, and they completely ignore the expense. The result is that patients may seek out medical care when they do not really need it. Providers, who are taught to provide any medical service that has even a remote chance of helping the patient, provided it does no harm, are only happy to oblige. Not only that, providers can raise their prices without worrying that insured patients will take their business elsewhere. Economists say that the resulting increases in health care costs are due to *moral hazard*.

The theory of moral hazard depends on the ubiquity of health insurance. In this regard, the theory is on solid footing.

All Canadians are covered under insurance programs operated by the provinces and funded jointly by the provincial and federal government. The NHS covers all Britons. Most Germans are covered by "sickness funds" which are organized by region, occupation, or company, but funded through government revenues generated by a payroll tax. The government-sponsored *Assurance Maladie* covers all French citizens. The French even have their own *Carte Vitale* (health credit card) they can use to charge services to the government. Nearly 9 out of 10 French purchase additional insurance to cover services not covered by the national health plan. Supplemental plans are also available, though less popular, in England and Germany. The Japanese national health system supplements corporate health insurance schemes; together, they pay for about half of all of Japan's health expenditures. The government insurance plans in all of these nations cover a wide range of health care services, including hospital and physician services, prescription drugs, and even spa treatments (in Germany) and fitness clubs (in Japan).

The United States has the largest gaps in coverage. While virtually all the elderly are covered under Medicare, about 20 percent of the nonelderly lack health insurance altogether. Medicare, Medicaid, and private insurance cover most services, but there are a few gaps in coverage. Medicare does not cover prescription drugs, though many seniors obtain private insurance for drugs. Coverage for some "nontraditional" services such as mental health care and acupuncture also varies by plan. Despite these gaps, most Americans are covered for most health care purchases, and the elderly, who tend to have the greatest medical needs, also have some of the most generous coverage.

There is no doubt that when most patients receive medical care, someone else almost always pays. The theory of moral hazard says that this arrangement leads to excessive expenditures. For a long time, the medical community refused to accept the theory. Critics correctly pointed out that patients rarely "buy" health care services in the same way they buy televisions, clothing, food, or most other goods and services.

Patients may occasionally ask for a specific drug or diagnostic test, but usually they let their providers make the medical decisions. Thus, moral hazard is not as simple as giving patients blank checks to buy whatever they want. If moral hazard exists, then at least one of three things must occur. Either (1) patients with insurance are more likely to visit their providers in the first place, (2) providers tend to recommend more costly service when their patients have insurance, or (3) insured patients are more likely to consent to their providers' recommendations.

Providers offered reasons to doubt whether any of these conditions would hold. They responded as follows: (1) Patients with minor aches and pains might let cost stand in the way of a provider visit, but surely a patient with serious medical needs would seek attention no matter what. (2) Providers themselves base their recommendations on medical science, not economics. (3) Patients almost always consent to recommended services, so it seems doubtful that insurance would matter. If these arguments are correct, then moral hazard must be very small.

Beginning in the 1960s, economic research studies indicated that moral hazard might be rather substantial. Patients who were required to pay a portion of the medical bill (known as a copayment) purchased far fewer medical services than those who received free care. The French used this argument to justify a 20 percent copayment (or *ticket modérateur*) in their national health system. In 1970, U.S. Senator Ted Kennedy and Congressman Wilbur Mills used the concept of moral hazard to defend their national health insurance proposal, which relied on copayments for cost containment. Despite the growing evidence of moral hazard, the medical community was still not convinced. Medical researchers noted that the economic studies of moral hazard did not involve randomized controlled trials, which is the gold standard of medical research. Moreover, economic estimates of the magnitude of moral hazard varied widely.

In 1977, an important study by Anne Scitovsky and Nelda McCall helped persuade some of the doubters that moral hazard was real.[3] Scitovsky and McCall found that Stanford University employees curtailed their use of the Palo Alto Medical Clinic by 25 percent after Stanford imposed a modest copayment. This is a tantalizingly large reduction in utilization. It is impossible to extrapolate this to entire health economy, but if copayments could reduce utilization by just 5 percent, the annual cost savings in the U.S. economy alone would be in the tens of billions of dollars.

Although this study had some limitations—it examined a small group of patients who visited one provider group and lacked a true randomized design—it convinced some skeptics that moral hazard was real. Just a few years later, the publication of the findings of the RAND National Health Insurance Experiment removed any lingering doubt.

THE RAND STUDY

The Kennedy-Mills national health insurance proposal relied on copayments to control costs. Despite years of economic research, no one had any idea how big the copayments needed to be or how much money could be saved. Although the Kennedy-Mills proposal died in Congress in 1972, interest in the use of copayments continued. In 1974, Congress funded the $83 million RAND National Insurance Experiment to find out, once and for all, the magnitude of moral hazard.

The RAND study was a remarkable piece of economic research. RAND conducted a massive social science experiment, in which thousands of people were randomly assigned to different insurance plans. The RAND plans covered virtually all medical services and reimbursed providers for their billed charges. The plans differed in just one important way—the level of coinsurance. For some study participants, all medical care was free. Others paid 25 percent of the cost. Some participants paid for nearly all their care until they reached a "catastrophic ceiling." (RAND paid for any expenses above the ceiling.) By randomizing at the start of the study, and employing additional statistical controls later on, RAND avoided the criticism leveled at earlier studies of moral hazard. Any differences in utilization between participants in the "free-care" plan and participants who made copayments would be irrefutable evidence of moral hazard.

RAND published its results in the early 1980s. The findings were startling. The cost of caring for patients in the free-care plan exceeded the cost of caring for the patients in the various cost-sharing plans by 30 percent. RAND had shown that moral hazard was real, and really big. The natural conclusion was that a simple and effective way to contain health care costs would be to require patients to share in the cost of care. Even modest copayments might reduce expenditures by as much as 10 to 30 percent.

But critics of the theory of moral hazard were still concerned. What if the patients making copayments were going without necessary services? If this was the case, then what economists called moral hazard might, in fact, be worthwhile medical care. Perhaps costs are higher when patients get free care, but if patients are better off, then the higher costs might be worthwhile. RAND had an answer to these critics as well.

RAND did not just measure medical costs. RAND also measured the health of study participants. The study looked at 11 health measures in 4 categories: general health, health habits, physiologic health, and the risk of dying. On virtually all measures, such as physical functioning (e.g., the ability to climb up stairs), mental health (e.g., frequency of depression), and risk of dying, there were no differences between the health of those receiving free care and those making copayments. Taken together, the RAND results indicate that free care is very costly but provides little in the way of health care benefits. The RAND study vindicated the theory of moral hazard. A lot of money is wasted when patients do not have to pay for medical care.

DEMAND INDUCEMENT

Being a cynical bunch, economists have agonized over another troubling feature of the health care system. Physicians play several roles in medicine. They must diagnose their patients' ailments, recommend treatments, and carry them out. Because physicians' income might depend on the number of treatments they perform, they have a potential conflict of interest. A physician who is paid for each treatment might be tempted to recommend a treatment of questionable value. Economists called this *demand inducement*.

We are all familiar with demand inducement in markets outside medicine. We are suspicious when an auto mechanic tells us we need new brakes or when a plumber tells us we need new pipes. Naturally, we are much more likely to trust our physicians. But is the trust always well placed? Is it possible that physicians might occasionally place their own financial interests above the well-being of their patients? Beginning in the 1970s, that is what economists aimed to learn.

Canadian economist Robert Evans published one of the first inducement studies in 1974, followed by a seminal study by Stanford economist Victor Fuchs in 1978.[4] Fuchs found that when surgeons' incomes were threatened by competition, they induced patients to undergo more surgery. In Fuchs' study, physicians responded to a 10 percent reduction in income by inducing 3 percent more surgery. This was not enough to fully restore their lost income, but enough to cause medical bills to increase substantially. Later studies generally confirmed the Fuchs findings, though there was some disagreement about the extent of inducement. Today, most economists accept that such inducement exists both in the United States and abroad, though many economists believe the magnitude of the problem is small. Many policy makers believe the problem is large, however, and Chapter 3 describes some of the steps that European nations and Canada have taken to limit the consequences of inducement.

In the United States, the theory of inducement encouraged HMOs to sever the link between utilization and compensation. Some HMOs, including Kaiser Permanente and the Group Health Cooperative (GHC) of Puget Sound, two of the oldest and largest, pay physicians a fixed salary. In Kaiser's words, this plan creates a "reversal of economics" designed to reduce expenditures.[5] The RAND study provided evidence about the effects of these salary arrangements on utilization. RAND randomly assigned several hundred individuals to the GHC. Medical utilization by these individuals was comparable to that in the highest cost-sharing indemnity plans and 30 percent below utilization in the free plan. Other studies confirm that the switch from fee-for-service payment to more restrictive forms of compensation can sharply curtail utilization.

BAD BUYS IN HEALTH CARE

Payers use the theories of moral hazard and demand inducement to curtail health care expenditures. Even with a cap on spending, there is no guarantee that health care dollars will be wisely spent. In 1967, the U.S. Department of Health, Education and Welfare reviewed a series of studies of treatments for kidney disease. They concluded that kidney transplants saved more life-years per dollar than did dialysis. Even so, political considerations led Congress to enact legislation favoring dialysis. To this day, doubts remain about the cost-effectiveness of dialysis. Examples like this are just the tip of the iceberg.

A recent, far-reaching report by Tammy Tengs and her colleagues at the Harvard School of Public Health identifies many questionable ways in which the public spends money to save lives.[6] The report's title, "Five-Hundred Life-Saving Interventions and Their Cost-Effectiveness," speaks of its breadth. In it, Tengs and her colleagues review literally thousands of cost-effectiveness research studies. They do not restrict their attention to medical interventions but also examine public health, safety, and pollution control.

Their findings are astonishing. Of the 500 interventions they study, dozens can be considered "bargains." A few interventions, including childhood immunization and, driving schools for bad drivers, save both lives and money by preventing more costly problems. Other "best buys" include prenatal care, flu vaccinations, chlorinating water, beta-blocker therapy after a heart attack, and in-home smoke detectors. These interventions cost just a few thousand dollars for each year of life saved.

Many interventions offer middle-of-the-road value. Kidney transplants cost $19,000 per life-year (versus $43,000 for dialysis), coronary bypass surgery costs $26,000, and flashing lights at railroad crossings cost $42,000. Unfortunately, many interventions, especially safety and pollution interventions, cost far more than this. Eliminating household radon costs $141,000, asbestos control costs $1.8 million, and chloroform emission standards at pulp mills $99 billion per life-year saved. Tengs identifies some relatively costly health care interventions as well. Endoscopies and X-rays to detect gastric cancer cost $420,000 and intensive care for patients with gastrointestinal bleeding costs $950,000 per life-year.

Tengs might also have reported on any number of anecdotal examples of extraordinary expenditures. In one well-publicized case, Children's Hospital of Philadelphia performed a $1 million procedure to separate Siamese twins. The physicians knew that one twin would die certainly and the other would have just a 1 percent chance of survival. The surviving infant died less than a year after the surgery, for a cost of $1 million per life-year. The chief surgeon at Children's Hospital defended the procedure, arguing that it is always worth trying to save a life, no matter what the cost.[7] He called this the *rescue principle.*

Does the rescue principle offer the best approach to saving lives? The $1 million that Children's Hospital spent on separating the Siamese twins might instead have been used to expand access to neonatal intensive care or to fund prenatal care. At a cost of $2,000 per year of life saved, this alternate would have saved 500 life-years. Another study coauthored by Tammy Tengs suggests that broad application of such a rational approach to medical decision making could save 60,000 lives annually in the United States alone, at no extra cost.[8]

We could save even more lives if we considered scaling back large government programs. For example, suppose we cut back spending on asbestos removal by $10 million. This decision would adversely affect the health of some people, with a total loss of about 5 life-years. But if we were to use that money to fund additional beta-blocker therapy, we could add 5,000 additional life-years, according to the Tengs study. We would realize a net gain of 4,995 life-years at no additional cost! Some might object to cutting back on asbestos removal on the grounds that a few million dollars is a small price to pay to save lives (a claim I will examine later on). But this objection is surely muted if the money saved by cutting back on asbestos removal goes to other interventions that save many more lives.

Others might object that there is no guarantee the money taken from asbestos removal programs, or from Children's Hospital, for that matter, would be used for other health programs. They are correct; such promises are almost impossible to keep. But why should health programs always have the first claim on spending? True, $10 million might buy 5 life-years if spent on asbestos removal, but as Victor Fuchs reminds us, it could also buy "justice, beauty, and knowledge" or whatever else we choose to spend the money on. Ultimately, we will have to decide whether it is worth giving up $10 million worth of other goods and services to gain 5 life-years. Chapter 8 will take a closer look at this thorny question.

THE WENNBERG VARIATIONS

Why do we make such cost-ineffective decisions? In the case of dialysis, the reason is partly due to politics. The case of the Siamese twins may just be a manifestation of moral hazard or demand inducement. But sometimes, physicians are simply guilty of questionable medical decision making. The best evidence of this emerged over 30 years ago, in work by Dartmouth physician Jack Wennberg.

Starting in the late 1960s, Wennberg grabbed the attention of the health care community by reporting on curious regional variations in care. In one famous study, he showed that the rates of some procedures, such as coronary bypass surgery, were much higher in New Haven than in Boston, but rates for other procedures, such as carotid endarterectomy, were much higher in Boston.[9] Other studies have documented similar variations throughout the United States, Canada, and Europe. There are even variations within a given community and among doctors at a given hospital. Differences in insurance and income cannot explain these "Wennberg variations." The bottom line is that the treatment you receive may depend as much on where you live and which provider you visit as it does on your medical condition.

Practice variations arise, in part, because medical providers have different training and experience, a fact that translates into different treatment styles. Some providers favor aggressive surgical interventions while others prefer a wait-and-see approach. Some are more partial to drug therapy than others. There is nothing necessarily wrong with these different approaches. Some surgeons are better than others and ought to be more aggressive. Some internists do a better job of monitoring side effects and ought to prescribe more drugs. Even when two physicians have equal skills, there is enough ambiguity in medicine so that they can disagree about the best way to treat a patient, and neither can be proved wrong.

But most policy analysts believe that the magnitude of practice variations is excessive. They believe that practice variations often reflect inappropriate medical decisions, rather than honest differences of opinion, and can cost billions of dollars and thousands of lives. Some variations are clearly unwarranted, such as variations in the rate of prescription of beta-blockers and aspirin therapy to heart attack victims. (The rate ought to be nearly 100 percent.) Other variations expose patients to dangerous yet unnecessary surgery, as appears to be the case for caesarian sections and prostatectomies.

DEFENDING RATIONING

Moral hazard, demand inducement, and practice variations form the theoretical foundation for rationing. If physicians and patients succumb to these problems, then maybe a little paternalism is in order. Rationing might cut a few percentage points off health care spending without jeopardizing outcomes. With a few billion saved here and there, soon you are talking about substantial savings!

Indeed, payers around the world use these concepts as excuses for restricting access to drugs and medical technology, and limiting certain surgical interventions while encouraging others. The problem faced by payers is that medical science continues to generate new and more costly products. Whether these are drugs that treat previously incurable diseases or techniques that open up new opportunities for surgical intervention, these medical advances have the potential to drain health care budgets. Unfortunately, neither payers nor providers have been sensible enough to realize that although some additional medical spending is absolutely warranted, other expenditures really are wasteful. The result, as detailed in Chapter 3, is a global regulatory mess that serves neither patients nor taxpayers.

ENDNOTES

1. Princeton economist Uwe Reinhardt first offered this provocative argument.

2. J. Williamson, 1991, "Medical Quality Management Systems in Perspective," in J. B. Couch, ed., *Health Care Quality Management for the 21st Century*, Tampa, FL: American College of Physician Executives, pp. 23–72.

3. A. Scitovsky and N. McCall, 1977, "Coinsurance and the Demand for Physician Services: Four Years Later," *Social Security Bulletin* 35(6): 3–19.

4. R. Evans, 1974, "Supplier-Induced Demand," in M. Perlman, ed., *The Economics of Health and Medical Care*, London: MacMillan. V. Fuchs, 1978, "The Supply of Surgeons and the Demand for Operations," *Journal of Human Resources* 13(supplement): 35–56.

5. C. Cutting, 1971, "Historical Development and Operating Concepts," in A. Somers, ed., *The Kaiser-Permanente Medical Program*, New York: Commonwealth Fund.

6. T. Tengs et al., 1995, "Five-Hundred Life-Saving Interventions and Their Cost-Effectiveness," *Risk Analysis* 15(3): 369–89.

7. R. Dworkin, "The Price of Life: How High the Cost Before It Becomes Too High?" *Los Angeles Times* 29 August 1993, Part M, p. 1.

8. T. Tengs and J. Graham, 1996, "The Opportunity Costs of Haphazard Social Investments in Life Saving" in R. Hahn, ed., *Risks, Costs, and Lives Saved: Getting Better Results from Regulation.*

9. J. Wennberg, J. Freeman, and W. Culp, 1987, "Are Hospital Services Rationed in New Haven or Overutilised in Boston?" *Lancet,* pp. 1185–88.

3 RATIONING AROUND THE WORLD

Some simple statistics demonstrate the extent of health care rationing around the world. Table 3.1 reports health care spending in the United States and other nations for 1998.[1] The nations in this comparison group are among the biggest spenders in the world—rationing is even more severe elsewhere. The table shows that the United States spends a far higher percentage of its GDP on health care than does any other nation, and a far higher amount per capita than any other nation. Part of this difference can be explained by higher prices in the United States. But another reason the United States spends more on medical care is that Americans use more medical care services.

TABLE 3.1   International Comparison of Health Care Spending

NATION	SPENDING AS PERCENTAGE OF GDP	SPENDING PER CAPITA
Australia	8.6	$1,718
Canada	9.3	$1,850
France	9.4	$2,324
Germany	10.3	$2,697
United Kingdom	6.8	$1,636
United States	12.9	$4,165

Digging a bit deeper into the data reveals some key differences in utilization. There are few international differences in access to physicians or hospital beds; in fact, patients in nations such as Canada and Germany see their physicians more often than do Americans. However, there are substantial differences in access to costly medical technologies. Table 3.2 reports the most recent data on the availability and use of three important technologies—MRI, open-heart surgery, and kidney dialysis.[2] The table shows that Americans have far higher access and utilization.

TABLE 3.2   Availability and Use of Medical Technology

NATION	MRI MACHINES PER MILLION PEOPLE	OPEN-HEART SURGICAL PROCEDURES PER 100,000 PEOPLE	KIDNEY DIALYSIS PATIENTS PER 100,000 PEOPLE
Australia	4.7	86	30
Canada	2.5	62	40
France	2.5	35	37
Germany	6.2	38	53
United Kingdom	3.4	41	27
United States	7.6	223	74

The data in Table 3.2 represent just the tip of the iceberg. Americans have greater access to transplants, hip replacements, radiation oncology, and many other costly high-tech interventions. In a similar way, Americans have greater access to medical specialists: There are about twice as many specialists per capita in the United States versus most other developed nations. When policymakers talk about rationing outside the United States, they usually mean rationing of access to medical specialists and the high-tech care they provide.

Supporters of nationalized health systems do not apologize for rationing. They cite the inherent inefficiency of an open-ended system plagued by moral hazard, practice variations, and, especially, demand inducement. It is difficult to overstate the extent to which overseas policymakers believe in inducement theory. I have heard European policymakers discuss inducement as though it were woven into the fabric of the medical care system. The policies of national health systems, such as the French *Assurance Maladie*, are firmly based on the assumption that suppliers can induce demand.[3] Limits on the training of specialists are also rooted in inducement theory. In the past decade, European and Canadian economists have written virtually every inducement article published in academic journals. Canada's leading health economist, Robert Evans, is a major proponent of inducement theory. With such fervent belief in inducement theory, it is no surprise that Canada and European nations ration access to medical services. In their view, to do otherwise would be to invite wasteful spending.

There is some indirect evidence that the high health care spending in the United States is wasteful. It is well known that Americans fare no better on gross health status measures such as life expectancy and infant mortality than do their counterparts in other developed nations. This suggests that the Americans' profligate spending is producing little health benefit. But health status measures are difficult to interpret because they reflect differences in lifestyles as well as differences in utilization. Perhaps utilization levels in the United States are appropriate and the rest of the world needs to spend more. Though there is no way to know for sure, I will have more to say about this debate in Chapter 9.

Even if U.S. spending is wasteful, due to inducement or other causes, it is quite a leap to conclude that government-sponsored rationing is the solution. As we will see, government rationing usually does not address the sources of market inefficiencies, including the much-feared demand inducement. The resulting policies may do more harm than good.

The rest of this chapter takes a closer look at rationing around the world. There is a rule of thumb when comparing national health care systems: When you have seen one system, you have seen one system. Thus, we will examine one national health system at a time. Our tour begins in Germany, crosses the pond to Canada, and finishes with another look at rationing in England.

RATIONING IN GERMANY

In some ways, the German health care system resembles the American health care system prior to the growth of managed care. Nearly 90 percent of Germans obtain health insurance coverage through private sickness funds, which cover virtually all health care services (including spa treatments!). Most physicians in Germany are self-employed and are paid on a fee-for-service basis. Likewise, hospitals are privately owned and are reimbursed on either a per diem or per discharge basis.[4] Health care costs in Germany are second only to those in the United States. Germany equals or surpasses the United States on several indicators of utilization, such as physician visits and hospitalizations per capita.

But appearances are deceiving. Germans may obtain insurance from private sickness funds and receive care from independent providers, but only under strict rules set by the government. Centralization is necessary to meet the objectives of the Cost-Containment Act of 1977. This act contains the *Konzertierte Aktion*, which established the principle of income-proportional financing. This means that the rate of growth of health care expenditures is supposed to be no higher than the growth of total wages. Though not legally binding, the *Konzertierte Aktion* has moral force and has driven regulatory actions ever since. For example, physicians and hospitals may be independent, but they are not free to set their own prices. Instead, regional governments mediate price negotiations between the sickness funds and representatives of provider groups. The result is uniform pricing within each region.

Many Germans laud uniform pricing for its fairness, but it leads to rationing in a variety of forms. For example, uniform pricing forces even the best hospitals and physicians to charge the same price as everyone else. As a result, Germans covered by sickness funds must queue for the best-quality providers. By way of contrast, the best providers in the United States limit the size of this queue by charging higher prices, resulting in rationing by willingness to pay. The same sort of price rationing now appears to be happening in Germany, though in a subtler form. High-income Germans may bypass sickness funds and purchase unregulated health insurance. About one-third of eligible Germans do so, and their ranks are slowly growing. Although providers must accept the uniform fee from sickness funds, they are free to charge whatever they wish to privately insured Germans. By opting out of sickness funds and purchasing unregulated health insurance, wealthy Germans can gain quicker access to the best physicians and hospitals.

Uniform pricing not only has led to queuing and a growing private insurance system but also has discouraged physicians from incurring the expenses necessary to improve their skills, hire nurses, purchase new equipment, and adopt information technologies. By the same token, German hospitals have little financial incentive to provide superior amenities. But they can and do charge higher prices to privately insured patients seeking private rooms. This is another "perk" afforded to Germans who bypass sickness funds.

Rationing takes other forms. An important element of the German system is that the prices negotiated between sickness funds and providers are not set in stone. Each region sets an overall cap on physician expenditures. If total payments to physicians exceed the cap, the fees are ratcheted down. The result is that physicians "churn" patients—seeing more and more patients for shorter amounts of time. With physicians billing for more visits, visit fees fall. Even physicians who are reluctant to compromise their practice styles feel obliged to churn patients, lest they see a loss in income resulting from churning by everyone else!

To prevent churning, the government profiles physician practice patterns. Physicians who prescribe too many treatments may undergo time-consuming audits and are subject to financial penalties. This system of oversight resembles utilization review controls and physician-profiling practices of U.S.

managed care organizations. In 1996, the German government augmented profiling with legislation known as *Neuordnungsgesetze* (NOG). The NOG caps physician billings for individual patients. This helps to limit the number of times a physician can churn each patient. Even so, audits and the NOG have had only limited success. Compared with their American counterparts, Germans visit their doctors about 15 percent more often.[5] Many office visits in Germany involve little more than a cursory interaction between physician and patient, just enough to generate a bill.

Another peculiar feature of the German system is the sharp division between hospital-based physicians and all other physicians. Only the former may treat patients in hospitals. This adversely affects continuity of care and has harmed efforts to implement U.S.-style managed care. The system also gives each group of physicians powerful incentives to provide as much care as possible on their own turf. The law was recently amended to permit hospital-based physicians to provide some postdischarge outpatient care, but such care is tightly regulated and the new law has led to few changes in practice.

Another form of rationing affects hospitals. Sickness funds cover only operating expenses. Hospitals rely on their regional governments to pay for capital expenses. Driven by the *Konzertierte Aktion* to cap overall expenditures, regional governments hold their purse strings tightly. While there is no shortage of hospital beds, the availability of technology is rationed, as was seen in Table 3.2. Despite this apparent lack of new technology, there are no waiting lists for care in Germany. This situation may reflect the chilling influence of physician profiling. After all, there cannot be waiting lists for services if German physicians do not prescribe them.

CONTROLLING DRUG COSTS IN GERMANY

By the late 1980s, Germany had the highest level of per capita drug expenditures in Europe. Drug use in Germany was average, so the high spending was due solely to high prices.

The German solution was to regulate prices though a system known as *reference pricing*.

Under reference pricing, all drugs are lumped into clusters based on therapeutic equivalence. For example, anti-ulcer medications such as Zantac and Tagamet are placed in the same cluster. Regulators then set a single price—the reference price—for all drugs in the cluster. In Germany, the reference price caps the amount that sickness funds may pay to drugmakers. The drugmakers are free to price above the cap, provided that patients pay the difference. In practice, however, most drug companies set a price exactly equal to the reference price.

In its first few years, the reference pricing system reduced the prices of regulated drugs by as much as 20 percent.[6] Yet spending on prescription drugs in Germany increased soon thereafter. The main reason was that the reference pricing system applied only to drugs with therapeutic equivalents. As drugmakers launched innovative new products, they were free to set their own prices. They increased sales efforts to encourage physicians to prescribe these more expensive drugs and lobbied regulators to classify their drugs as truly innovative, rather than cluster them with low-priced competitors. Pharmacoeconomic research was vitally important to bolstering these claims. Though lobbying efforts often paid off, they also led to unnecessary delays in product launches. Germans might have to wait months for regulators to establish reference prices for drugs that had been approved under rules of safety and efficacy.

Recent regulatory changes have minimized the importance of reference pricing in Germany. In 1996, Germany gave up trying to control the prices of patented drugs and restricted reference pricing to drugs that have gone off patent. A lower court has recently questioned the constitutionality of reference pricing, and the European Court of Justice is set to rule in 2003 as to whether reference pricing violates European competition laws.

As reference pricing weakens, regulators have turned to other mechanisms for reducing drug expenditures. The NOG requires Germans to make copayments for drugs (as well as for hospital stays, physical therapy, and other services). According to one report, the copayments reduce drug purchases by 10 percent.[7] The NOG also caps drug expenditures by physicians. For example, gynecologists may spend only about DM 75 (about $40) on drugs per patient per year, and they must make up the difference out of their own pockets.[8] Even more ambitious drug regulations are on the horizon. Since 1993, German regulators have been at work developing a "positive list" of drugs that the sickness funds may pay for. The positive list would move Germany closer to England's NICE by using explicit cost-effectiveness measures for drug approval.

IF IT LOOKS LIKE RATIONING...

In 1980, German health care expenditures accounted for 8 percent of the GDP, just a shade below spending in the United States. By 1990, spending in the United States had grown to 10.2 percent of GDP. But in Germany, spending stood at just 8.4 percent. Today, spending in Germany is just above 10 percent of GDP, versus about 14 percent in the United States. The guiding principle of *Konzertierte Aktion* has successfully kept a lid on health care spending. But in the process, it has also profoundly reshaped the practice of medicine.

German physicians must balance the incentives to churn under the price caps with incentives to hold down utilization under the NOG. At the same time, outpatient and inpatient physicians continue to protect their turf. Despite two decades of government-sponsored rationing, Germans remain concerned about rising health care costs. Many fear that further regulation, such as the creation of positive lists for drugs, will hurl their system toward bureaucratic chaos and additional rationing. According to one recent survey, most Germans believe that they will eventually have to live without many drugs that they are used to obtaining on demand.[9]

RATIONING IN CANADA

Perhaps because the United States and Canada are neighbors, there is an enormous debate about the relative virtues of their health care systems. Supporters of the Canadian system observe that it spends about 40 percent less per capita on health care, yet every Canadian is covered, copayments are nil, and Canadians are just as healthy as or healthier than Americans. Supporters of the U.S. system counter that Canadians face significant barriers to access that lead to measurable health problems. Both sides are correct.

The origins of the Canadian health care system date back to the 1950s, when the federal government agreed to subsidize provincial hospital insurance programs. By 1961, all the provinces were offering such programs. A decade later, the provinces added coverage for physician services. The Canadian system took its current form under the Canada Health Act of 1984. Under this legislation, the federal government pays for roughly half the cost of the provincial programs. In exchange, the provinces must implement rules and regulations that remove financial and other barriers to access to health services.[10] Provinces are supposed to pay for all "medically necessary" services, but the act does not define what is medically necessary.[11]

There are some differences across provincial programs (e.g., British Columbia uses a reference pricing plan for prescription drugs, whereas Ontario uses QALYs to negotiate prices with drugmakers). However, rationing stems from several features that the plans hold in common. First, all Canadians are fully covered for a wide package of benefits. There is essentially no price rationing, and most Canadians are very proud of this egalitarian system (though support has wavered in the past decade). Second, the provinces reimburse physicians on a fee-for-service basis. The provinces have curtailed fee increases, and, despite advances in technology and training, increases in fees barely keep pace with inflation. The results are much like those in Germany—an increase in the number of physician visits. Finally, the provinces set hospital budgets, strictly limiting the purchase of costly medical technologies. This combination of zero cost, demand inducement, and limited supply of medical technology has resulted in long waits for a wide range of medical services.[12]

Canadians generally have excellent access to primary care physicians (PCPs), but they still have to wait slightly longer than Americans for an appointment.[13] Once patients get to a PCP's office, the real waiting begins. Canadians have a difficult time getting referrals to specialists, often waiting two weeks or longer (versus a few days in the United States). Once they get to their specialists, Canadians may have to wait several months or more for tests and procedures that can be obtained on demand in the United States (though perhaps after a few hassles from HMOs).

Canada's defenders argue that waiting lists are necessary for cost containment, and they point to surveys showing that most Canadians are very satisfied with their health care system. Not only do Canadians tell pollsters they are happy, but they also "vote with their feet" in support of the Canadian system. Surprisingly few Canadians ever travel south to the United States for care. One recent study found that the number of Canadians crossing the border for health care was "infinitesimal" when compared with number receiving care in Canada.[14]

THE CONSEQUENCES OF WAITING LISTS

Public opinion aside, studies show that rationing is taking its toll on the health of Canadians. As the provinces struggle with efforts to keep health care costs under 10 percent of GDP, rationing intensifies and waiting lists grow. For patients, the results can be deadly. One study found that many patients awaiting heart valve surgery faced waits of 90 days or longer, and about 1 percent of them died—many needlessly—while waiting.[15] Another study looked at the treatment of patients who have had heart attacks. It found that Americans received much more aggressive medical care than did Canadians, with higher rates of cardiac catheterization and coronary bypass surgery.[16] The results were tangible. One year following their heart attacks, Americans were in significantly better physical and mental health and were much more likely to have returned to normal activities.

Rationing is not confined to heart care. A disturbing study found that more than one-third of patients recommended for hip replacement surgery had to wait a year or longer for their new hips.[17] About one-third of these patients reported a high level of pain and difficulty functioning normally. Yet another study estimated that half of the patients who could benefit from kidney dialysis were not receiving treatment.[18] The studies go on and on. A recent study found that the median waiting time for radiation oncology, cardiovascular surgery, and neurosurgery exceeded the clinically reasonable wait times.[19] Eighty percent of Albertans reported that they expected to wait for necessary health care services; about half of those who did wait reported extra stress and worsening pain.[20] Forty percent became depressed while waiting. Residents of Saskatchewan face an average wait of 40 weeks for elective surgery.[21]

It is difficult to square the facts of rationing with public opinion. A decade ago, a Canadian physician published a study showing that waiting times for cancer treatment were three times as long as in the United States. When asked about lengthy waits, he indicated that if he had cancer, he would go to Buffalo, New York, to get prompt treatment.[22] Yet he also steadfastly supported the Canadian system.

THE FUTURE OF RATIONING IN CANADA

Rationing is necessary in Canada for the simple reason that provincial governments have not been willing to spend enough money to prevent it. As some Canadian physicians have noted, this strategy puts patient interests squarely at odds with the interests of the provincial governments, because each time a patient needs costly medical care, provincial budgets go deeper in the red.[23] But the provinces are finding it increasingly difficult to keep to their budgets without antagonizing their citizens, and the once near-unanimous support for the national health system is beginning to waver. As waiting lists grow, regulators may begin to question the wisdom of maintaining such tight controls on health care spending.

RATIONING IN ENGLAND

The postcode lottery and National Institute for Clinical Excellence (NICE), described in Chapter 1, are only the latest manifestations of rationing in England. Established in 1949 to assure health care to all Britons, the National Health Service (NHS) is the poster child (for better or for worse) of socialized medicine. The system, which has met its objective of providing virtually free care to all Britons, is funded entirely through income taxes. Nearly all health care providers work directly for the government, which owns almost all hospitals.

Like other government-funded systems, resources for the NHS are limited by tax collections. And as in other government-funded systems, British policymakers have been reluctant to allow health care to consume an increasing percentage of the total government budget. To make matters worse, the British have frozen spending at a level far below that in other nations. Since 1970, per capita spending on health care in Great Britain has been about 60 percent of that in Germany, France, and Canada, and less than 40 percent of spending in the United States. To keep spending down, the NHS has kept a lid on provider salaries and has been slow to embrace new technologies.

The inevitable result has been rationing. About 1 million Britons are currently on waiting lists for hospital care, with the average wait for admission approaching four months.[24] Nearly 50,000 patients must wait a year or more to get into a hospital. Once admitted, they may never get access to some high-tech services that are commonly available in the United States and elsewhere, such as MRIs or open-heart surgery. But rationing in England is not limited to costly medical technologies. Britons often must wait hours just to get into emergency rooms.[25] After finally getting into a hospital, patients may have to go on another waiting list for home care or a nursing home bed. One study found that at any given time, 3,000 elderly patients have been waiting at least 28 days to be discharged.[26] This delay just lengthens the queue for patients waiting for hospital admission.

Even access to primary care is restricted. On a per capita basis, there are only about 60 percent as many general practitioners in England as in other nations, and the physician deficit is growing. Demoralized by low salaries, low prestige, and growing regulatory burdens, senior English physicians increasingly opt for early retirement, while junior physicians increasingly wish they had chosen other careers.[27] Patients suffer the consequences. They wait to see their physicians, and when they do see them, the visits are very brief. In addition, an impending shortage of surgeons is likely to make hospital waiting lists grow even longer.

Patients on waiting lists are suffering. Newspapers routinely report accounts of patients dying while waiting for care. Although systematic research is only just emerging, initial studies have offered sobering evidence of the consequences of waiting lists. Two recent studies suggest that every year, 600 people in England and 50 in Scotland die while waiting for heart surgery.[28] Additional studies may show that waiting lists in England are causing far more harm than in Canada.

To cope with its budget woes, the NHS is constantly reinventing itself. Originally, the centralized system had all the hallmarks of an entrenched bureaucracy. Efficient providers saw their budgets slashed while inefficient providers got fatter and fatter. In the past decade, the NHS has reorganized physicians and hospitals into "trusts," with financial responsibility (through the same capitation-like incentives used by American HMOs) to provide care to their local communities. The NHS has also empowered local health authorities to shop around for the most efficient hospitals and trusts. These steps look a lot like U.S. managed care, but they have had only limited success. The local authorities lack the information necessary to identify the best providers, and they are under enormous pressure to ensure the survival of even the most inefficient local hospitals and trusts. Thus far, these problems have limited the effectiveness of economic incentives.

Through periods in which the national government has introduced economic incentives and other periods in which the government has reined them in, the budget crunch in the NHS has continued unabated. NICE, the latest attempt to deal with budget limitations, has issued only a few dozen guidances and has yet to materially affect the NHS budget. With rationing on the rise, the NHS continues to come under pressure to effect more sweeping reforms. The current Blair government has promised a massive infusion of new funds into the NHS, but for many Britons, it is too little, too late.

To avoid waiting lists, hundreds of thousands of wealthy Britons purchase private health insurance or pay for hospital care directly, giving them access to a handful of private hospitals and leading specialists. This practice has created the kind of two-tiered system that nationalized health care is supposed to avoid. The rest of Europe is taking notice. The French health minister decried NHS rationing as "medieval."[29] German officials have turned the problems in the NHS into an opportunity for German health providers. Germany has approved a team of doctors and nurses to convert a military hospital in Portsmouth, England, into an outpatient surgery center. But Germany is not just exporting providers. The German government is offering English patients special travel deals to Germany, including low airfares and discounted hospital stays.[30] The Germans will have to compete with French health care providers, however. "Vacation" packages to hospitals in the south of France are becoming increasingly popular among wealthy Britons tired of waiting for care.

RATIONING ELSEWHERE IN THE WORLD

Waiting lists, delays in getting drugs, and other forms of rationing are not limited to Germany, Australia, and England. The French may complain about the NHS, but at least the British do not have to make substantial copayments along the lines of the French *ticket modérateur*. Scandanavian countries limit access to new technologies. Surgery rates in Japan are one-third lower than in Europe and Canada. The Japanese also rely on fee schedules that have led to German-style patient churning and the requisite utilization restrictions. Even the United States, where spending seems profligate compared to the rest of the world, is far from immune to rationing, as Chapter 4 discusses.

ENDNOTES

1. This is the most recent year for which full data are available. See *OECD Health Data 2001: A Comparative Analysis of 30 Countries* (CD-ROM).

2. Data taken from G. Anderson and P. Hussey, 2001, "Comparing Health System Performance in OECD Countries," *Health Affairs* 20(3): 219–232. Updated from *OECD Health Data 2001: A Comparative Analysis of 30 Countries* (CD-ROM).

3. P. Lancry and S. Sandier, 1999, "Rationing Health Care in France," *Health Policy* 50: 23–38.

4. A shift from per diem to per discharge payments began in 1995. Per discharge payments are adjusted according to the patient's disease and treatment, using diagnosis-related groups (DRGs). This is the same system used by Medicare and many HMOs and PPOs in the United States.

5. *OECD Health Data 2001: A Comparative Analysis of 30 Countries* (CD-ROM).

6. See P. Danzon and H. Liu, 1997, "Reference Pricing and Physician Drug Budgets," working paper, Philadelphia, The Wharton School.

7. A. Salama, 2000, "Germany—Drugs and Pharmaceuticals," *National Trade Data Bank Market Reports.*

8. Ibid.

9. W. Kaesbach, 2001, "Pharmaceutical Policies in Germany and European Competition Law," paper prepared for the conference on *European Integration and Health Care Systems,* December 2001.

10. R. Wilson, M. Rowan, and J. Henderson, 1995, "Core and Comprehensive Health Services: Introduction to the Canadian Medical Association's Decision-Making Framework," *Canadian Medical Association Journal* 152(7): 1063–66.

11. Wilson et al., ibid.

12. It is somewhat difficult to interpret data on waiting times. Physicians may place patients on waiting lists in anticipation of future needs, and the provinces try to triage patients to minimize waits for those with the most urgent needs.

13. For more on these survey findings, see K. Donelan et al., "All Payer, Single Payer, Managed Care, No Payer: Patients' Perspectives in Three Nations," *Health Affairs* 15(2): 254–65.

14. S. Katz et al., 2002, "Phantoms in the Snow: Canadians' Use of Health Care Services in the United States," *Health Affairs* 21(3): 19–31.

15. C. Morgan, K. Sykora, and C. Naylor, 1998, "Analysis of Deaths While Waiting for Cardiac Surgery Among 29,293 Consecutive Patients in Ontario, Canada," *Heart*, 79: 345–49.

16. D. Mark et al., 1994, "Use of Medical Resources and Quality of Life after Acute Myocardial Infarction in Canada and the United States," *New England Journal of Medicine* 331(17): 1130–5.

17. J.I. Williams et al., 1997, "The Burden of Waiting for Hip and Knee Replacements in Ontario," *Journal of Evaluation in Clinical Practice* 3(1): 59–68.

18. C. Kjellstrand and H. Moody, 1994, "Hemodialysis in Canada: A First-Class Medical Crisis," Canadian Medical Association Journal 150(7): 1067–71.

19. Cited in "Heresy in Canada," Wall Street Journal (Editorial), 29 November 1999, p. A28.

20. "The Wait for Health Care Is Getting Longer," report by the Alberta Medical Association, 1999.

21. "Report Says Major Changes Needed for Saskatchewan Surgical Wait List System," Canadian Business and Current Affairs, 25 April 2001. Press release.

22. M. Walker, 1999, "The Americas: Canadians with Medical Needs Follow Their Doctors South," Wall Street Journal 5 March 1999, p. A15.

23. Kjellstrand and Moody, ibid.

24. J. Carvel, 2002, "Hospital Waiting List Rises by 22,700 Despite Extra Cash for NHS," The Guardian 8 June 2002.

25. B. Marsh, 2001, "NHS is Medieval, Says French Chief," London Daily Mail 5 October 2001, p. 15.

26. See M. Dean, 2002, "The NHS—The Problem Is Capacity, Not Funding," The Lancet 359(9311): 1043.

27. T. Dalrymple, 2002, "The Doctor's Tale: NHS in Crisis," New Statesman 4 February 2002.

28. See "Fatal Delay: The Human Cost of NHS Waiting Lists," Sunday Times 5 May 2002 and S. Leonard, "Hundreds of Scots Die Waiting for NHS Heart Treatment," Sunday Times 12 May 2002.

29. Marsh, ibid.

30. J. Hope, 2001, "In Need of a Hospital Bed? Try Germany," London Daily Mail 7 February 2001, p. 23.

4

RATIONING IN THE U.S. HEALTH CARE MARKETPLACE

Rationing of health care may grab headlines in England and Canada, but there is a long and controversial history of rationing in the United States. The U.S. health care system is a blend of public and private insurance, combined with largely private provision of care. Insurance coverage is not universal, and payers and providers use a myriad of financial incentives to influence utilization. The result is a health care system that spends more money per capita than anywhere else, yet fails to provide health insurance for 15 percent of the population.

The federal Medicare program provides blanket coverage for all elderly and disabled Americans, and the federal/state Medicaid programs provide coverage for many of the nation's poor. But most Americans under age 65 rely on private health insurance that they usually obtain through their employers. This means that there are gaps in coverage, especially for those under age 65. Many unemployed Americans do not qualify for Medicaid. Working Americans, especially part-time and seasonal workers and those who work at small firms, are not assured of employer-provided coverage. Some individuals who are unable to obtain employer-sponsored insurance may get coverage through a family member or may purchase an individual policy. But others balk at the high price of individual health insurance and prefer to remain uninsured.

RATIONING THROUGH THE MARKET MECHANISM: THE UNINSURED IN THE UNITED STATES

Approximately 40 million Americans do not have health insurance. These uninsured Americans tend to be younger and healthier than average, but about 10 million are children and millions more have chronic medical needs. When the uninsured need medical attention, a few are able to pay for it themselves. But most others rely on a safety net—charity care that is provided by the nation's nonprofit and government hospitals and by local community health providers.

The safety net is not enough to prevent rationing. The uninsured in the United States receive fewer medical services, and have to endure longer waits, than do those who have insurance. Rationing of the uninsured is likely to worsen. In the past, nonprofit hospitals relied on revenues from private insurers, Medicaid, and Medicare to subsidize care for the uninsured. Even then, the uninsured often had to wait to receive care and were less likely to receive the newest and most expensive treatments. Hospitals that care for a large number of the uninsured, known as *disproportionate share* hospitals, got a shot in the arm in the early 1990s when the federal government increased subsidies. But declining payments from HMOs, Medicare, and Medicaid are taking their toll on these hospitals. Some have been accused of "dumping" the uninsured—transferring them to government-owned hospitals that are often inconveniently located and inadequately funded.

Physicians in private practice are equally reluctant to treat the uninsured. As with hospitals, financial pressures have caused physicians to pay careful attention to the bottom line, and taking the time to treat the uninsured is an act of charity that many physicians believe they can no longer afford. Rapidly rising malpractice premiums are likely to make the situation even worse. Uninsured patients in need of primary care must then turn to local community health centers that, like government hospitals, are often underfunded.

The results of this market-based rationing are readily apparent. Many of the uninsured are diagnosed later in the course of illness, and, once diagnosed, they receive less intensive treatment. They are less likely to receive expensive new drugs or get access to highly trained specialists. Even so, the problem of access to medical care among the uninsured in the United States may be overstated. There is no definitive study to suggest that America's uninsured have poorer access to medical care then government-insured patients in other nations. Uninsured Americans may have shorter life expectancies, but this fact could be attributable to poverty and lifestyle rather than access to medical care.

ATTEMPTS TO PROVIDE UNIVERSAL COVERAGE

The number and percentage of uninsured Americans are at the highest levels since the early years of Medicare and Medicaid in the 1960s. In 1993, President Bill Clinton proposed legislation that would have provided nearly universal coverage. Most Americans supported the idea of universal coverage, as did leading medical groups such as the American Medical Association. Many large corporations, tired of paying for spiraling health insurance premiums, also backed the plan. Yet after nearly two years of hearings, expert panels, and heated debate, the Clinton plan died in Congress without coming up for a vote. This was hardly the first time that a national health insurance proposal was a central issue in Washington. Presidents Wilson, Truman, Johnson, and Nixon all offered plans for national health insurance. When Democrats controlled Congress in the early 1970s, a plan authored by Senator Ted Kennedy and Congressman Wilbur Mills seemed ready for passage, and in 1980, Republican congressional leaders crafted their own plan to expand coverage to all Americans.

They all failed. The Kennedy-Mills plan was tabled after the Washington, D.C., police found Congressman Mills cavorting in the Washington Mall reflecting pool with nightclub stripper Fanny Foxe. Presidents Truman and Nixon faced political crises that undermined their political effectiveness. Republicans criticized President Clinton's plan for its labyrinthine structure. But in the end, there was one common thread running through all of the failures. All the plans would require hefty increases in taxes. Thus far, the American public seems unwilling to use tax dollars to massively expand coverage to the uninsured.

Proponents of national health insurance in the United States claim that tax increases are unnecessary. The money would come, they claim, by eliminating the high administrative costs of managed care, and from the profits earned by investor-owned insurers and providers. Proponents of national health insurance view these expenses as wasteful. Regardless of the merits of this claim—costly administrative oversight may actually save money by reducing unnecessary utilization, and profits may attract entrepreneurs with new ideas for delivering care—the underlying premise is false. Careful analyses by the Congressional Budget Office continually show that a national health care system will cost tens of billions of additional dollars annually.

RATIONING AMONG INSURED AMERICANS

Perhaps supporters will one day muster enough votes for passage of universal health coverage, but they will not be able to eliminate rationing in America. Critics of the U.S. system are quick to accuse MCOs of rationing—an accusation that I will discuss later in this chapter. But even patients with generous indemnity insurance face barriers to access. For one thing, virtually all indemnity plans require copayments. We know from the RAND study discussed in Chapter 2 that copayments cause price rationing—even modest copayments can curtail utilization as much as 25 percent. The RAND study showed that most of this price rationing seems to involve a reduction in moral hazard utilization. This price rationing is probably a good thing, saving a lot of money with little to no risk to patients' health.

Patients with indemnity insurance may also face institutional barriers to care. Access may be hindered by geography (especially for rural patients seeking specialists and tertiary care hospitals), culture, and language. There is abundant research about all these barriers, and government agencies have spent billions of dollars to break them down.

Insured patients face one other barrier to care that is frequently overlooked. Most patients delegate medical decision-making authority to their physicians. As gatekeepers, physicians assure that their patients get access to whatever care they deem necessary. But gatekeepers sometimes close the gates. They may choose not to prescribe a certain drug that a patient requests, or not to recommend a requested procedure. They may refuse to admit their patients to certain hospitals, either for their own convenience or because of concerns about quality. Rather than seek out another physician, patients may go along with their own physician's advice. Reliance on physician discretion is tantamount to rationing.

Patients have good reason to entrust physicians with these life-and-death rationing decisions. Physicians have years of training and experience that most patients cannot match. Perhaps more important, patients believe their physicians to be compassionate, often placing patients' interests above their own. Physicians are not completely selfless, of course, but they are probably at least as altruistic as practitioners of any other profession.

Yet years of training and experience, combined with all the compassion in the world, cannot guarantee that physicians will always make the right decisions. Recent evidence on medical errors suggests that physicians are hardly infallible, and there is an ongoing effort to reduce the physician error rate. Prior to the recent concerns about medical errors, however, most concerns about medical decision making focused on costs. Physician gatekeepers were rarely accused of rationing. Quite the opposite was true. By the 1970s, analysts had begun to associate physician control with demand inducement and practice variations, and they further complained that physicians did little to contain moral hazard. As health care costs experienced double-digit growth year after year, policymakers decided that something had to be done to curtail the resulting inefficiencies.

GOVERNMENT-SPONSORED RATIONING IN THE UNITED STATES

For the past half-century, the conventional wisdom has been that the U.S. health care system is fraught with inefficiency. Policy makers have accepted the fact that eliminating inefficiency would almost surely require restricting the availability and use of services and would therefore be a form of rationing. But there has been substantial disagreement about how to go about such rationing.

During the 1970s, several state governments tried to stamp out waste through regulation. By far the most controversial regulations, known as certificate-of-need (CON) laws, attempted to block spending on hospital beds and equipment. To enforce CON laws, health care planners established targets for "efficient" utilization of hospital facilities. In theory, hospitals would not be allowed to spend money on new beds or equipment unless they met the targets. This strategy would reduce the available supply of services, thereby reducing utilization and costs. But the CON laws lacked teeth and did little to slow hospital expansion. Americans continued to have unfettered access to the latest and most expensive services.

Several states also tried to curtail spending by regulating hospital prices. These programs had modest success at best. New York State had the most restrictive price controls, slashing hospital payments for all patients, regardless of insurance. The price controls did slow the rate of growth of hospital prices by a little bit, but they also led to the closures of dozens of inner-city hospitals, forcing local residents to travel for care or go without. Other states slashed Medicaid payments to providers but did not regulate payments in the private sector. Medicaid patients soon had a hard time finding providers willing to take them, and they increasingly had to visit government-owned hospitals. One study of California's Medicaid program found that patients' access to vital coronary care services fell dramatically after the state cut provider payments. Hundreds of patients may have died as a result of the cutbacks.[1]

The modest cost savings resulting from price regulation encouraged the federal government to change the way it paid for Medicare hospitalizations. In 1983, Medicare switched from fee-for-service medicine and cost-based reimbursement to a sliding fee schedule. Under what is known as the prospective payment system (PPS), hospitals receive a fee for each admission that depends on the patient's medical condition, or diagnosis-related group (DRG). The theory behind the PPS was that a fee schedule would encourage hospitals to become more efficient because they would keep the savings. This plan would reverse the economic incentives inherent in the old system.

The switch to the PPS worked. There was an immediate decline in hospital inpatient costs. But the change in financial incentives caused providers to shift care to new settings, and their patients went along with them. Patient did not perceive that access to inpatient care was being rationed; nonetheless, rationing occurred, and outpatient utilization skyrocketed.

The Medicare program grew rapidly through the 1980s and 1990s. Faced with a budget shortfall, Medicare administrators began cutting payments to providers in the late 1990s. Not surprisingly, Medicare enrollees were soon having a taste of the access problems previously experienced by Medicaid enrollees. After a 5.4 percent reduction in physician fees in 2001, 17 percent of family physicians indicated that they would no longer accept new Medicare patients.[2] Access problems are not limited to primary care. Many specialists, including some of the best and highest-paid in their profession, are no longer seeing new Medicare patients. With Medicare fees set to fall an additional 11 percent by 2005, access problems are likely to worsen.

These experiences confirm a simple fact about health care providers. They may be altruistic, but financial incentives still matter. For the better part of the century, HMOs have exploited financial incentives to eliminate waste while maintaining reasonable levels of access.[3] Today, HMOs and other

MCOs combine financial incentives with several other policies to contain costs. In the process, they have become the subject of much scorn and derision.

A BRIEF HISTORY OF MANAGED CARE

The origins of HMOs can be traced to the late nineteenth century, when small groups of physicians provided industrial medicine for a prepaid fee per employee. By the 1940s, several prepayment arrangements were scattered across the country. The most prominent were the Kaiser Permanente Medical Group/Kaiser Foundation Health Plan and the Group Health Cooperative of Puget Sound (GHC). The medical establishment perceived that prepayment was a threat to professionalism, so local medical societies fought to deny hospital privileges to physicians who accepted prepayment. Ultimately, the courts tore down those barriers, permitting HMOs to grow and prosper.

In 1970, a young physician and health care consultant named Paul Ellwood coined the term *health maintenance organization* to describe these prepaid arrangements. The name was supposed to capture the idea that prepayment encouraged the organizations to prevent illness rather than just cure it. At a time when Americans were obsessed with reducing health care costs, HMOs became the darlings of the policy community. Blue Cross and Blue Shield Association President Walter McNerney encouraged local plans to experiment with HMOs, and prominent Stanford University Professor Alain Enthoven published two articles in the *New England Journal of Medicine* singing their praises.[4] President Nixon even made HMOs the centerpiece of his national health care proposal.[5] In 1978, University of California researcher Harold Luft published an influential article entitled "How Do HMOs Achieve Their 'Savings'?"[6] The article provided evidence that HMOs could reduce costs by as much as 40 percent, largely by reducing hospital utilization.

At this time, U.S. businesses were struggling to compete in a global economy. Threatened by rising health care costs and disenchanted with government cost controls, companies like

General Motors and 3M went looking for a solution. They found HMOs. HMOs expanded across the nation, followed by less restrictive preferred provider organizations (PPOs). By the mid-1990s, virtually all privately insured Americans were covered by some form of managed care.

There is unambiguous evidence that managed care sharply reduced the level of health care spending in the United States. Forecasts made in the early 1990s suggested that health care costs would reach 20 percent of GDP by 2000. Thanks to rising enrollments in managed care, that figure stayed below 14 percent, translating into an annual savings of as much as $300 billion. Costs are rising again, but from a much lower base. The massive savings generated by managed care appear to be permanent.

Although managed care has saved Americans billions of dollars, it has not won their trust. MCOs rank alongside tobacco companies as the least trustworthy American businesses. Many Americans equate managed care with rationing, and they accuse MCO executives of placing profits ahead of access. Of course, there has always been rationing in the U.S. health care system. The question is not whether MCOs ration but whether their form of rationing is worse than other forms. To answer this question, it is necessary to examine how MCOs cut costs.

MCO STRATEGIES FOR CONTAINING COSTS

The early supporters of prepaid group practices claimed that prepayment would eliminate physician incentives to induce demand or accommodate moral hazard utilization. Instead, physicians would respond to prepayment by providing fewer services, thereby driving down costs.[7] Critics countered that prepayment led to blatant rationing. They were both correct. But neither camp seemed willing to confront the trade-off between costs on the one hand and access and quality on the other. Supporters believed that moral hazard and demand inducement were so out of hand that any cutbacks were obviously beneficial. Opponents countered that access and quality must come first, regardless of the cost.

The RAND study of the GHC, detailed in Chapter 2, bolstered the position of the HMO supporters.[8] RAND found that the GHC patients had lower utilization and costs than indemnity patients. RAND also found no difference in outcomes. The GHC may have been rationing, but it was the right kind of rationing.

The RAND study was hardly reassuring to critics of HMOs. The GHC may have provided high-quality care, but it was a nonprofit HMO with a long history of serving its local community. Managed care growth in the 1980s and 1990s was dominated by new organizations owned by profit-seeking investors. On top of that, the pressure to contain costs had intensified, and MCOs were using new and more controversial techniques to limit utilization. Fears rose that HMOs would be doing the wrong kind of rationing.

Utilization Review (UR). In 1910, the Flexner Commission issued a historic report that established medicine in the United States as a scientifically based, self-regulating profession. Since then, physicians have enjoyed a great deal of autonomy. But this did not mean that each physician practiced in isolation. Quite the opposite was true. Professional Control is central to the practice of medicine. Physicians establish the standards for licensure and entry into specialty societies. Hospital staffs establish credentialing requirements. Even after physicians are licensed and credentialed, they continue to be subject to peer review. Hospital quality committees review medical charts to ensure that staff physicians deliver appropriate care. Committee members rely on their own experiences, but they also consult the latest evidence on best practices, helping the latest scientific advances find their way into practice.

Physicians may embrace peer review, but they have been loath to accept review by outsiders. Prior to managed care, physicians welcomed input from fellow members of the hospital staff and local specialty societies, but peer review from payers or consumer groups was unheard of. Physicians had such complete and utter control over decision-making in the hospital that the hospital chief of staff (a physician) was usually more powerful than the hospital president (a business manager).

This remarkable degree of autonomy began to fade in the 1970s. Rapid increases in Medicare and Medicaid costs, combined with a deepening understanding of the problems of moral hazard, gave the federal government a heightened interest in maintaining some oversight over the medical profession. When it enacted CON legislation, Congress also mandated the creation of 50 statewide professional standards review organizations (PSROs) and charged them with establishing guidelines for the delivery of medical care. Combining expert opinions with information from published research, PSROs developed guidelines for dozens of treatments, ranging from open-heart surgery to hospitalization for pneumonia. The guidelines specified the clinical indications for treatment and even recommended schedules for diagnosis, surgery, and discharge. But Congress did not give PSROs much in the way of enforcement power. With only the bully pulpit to effect change, PSROs were ineffective. Physician practice patterns, and costs, changed very little if at all.

PSROs may have had little direct impact on the practice of medicine, but they opened the door to further third-party intervention into the medical care process. As costs continued to mount, many private insurance companies began imposing their own utilization controls, often mimicking PSRO guidelines. To give these requirements some teeth, private insurers refused to reimburse providers for services rendered unless they obtained permission beforehand. There was soon a burgeoning market of firms providing these utilization review (UR) services.

Third-party UR got a big boost in 1983 with the introduction of the Medicare PPS. To ensure that providers would not abuse complex rules and regulations, Congress created professional review organizations (PROs). PROs are nonprofit organizations made up largely of members of their local medical communities. Congress required PROs to set specific goals for reducing health care utilization and costs and to perform the necessary UR activities to achieve these goals. For example, a PRO might set a goal of one coronary bypass procedure per 50,000 people. To achieve this goal, it would establish medical criteria for appropriateness. If a provider performed coronary bypass surgery that did not meet these criteria, the PRO could recommend that Medicare deny payment.

It did not take long for some of the larger PROs to offer UR services to private insurance companies. Private sector UR grew rapidly. By the mid-1990s, virtually every important medical decision in the United States had to be vetted by a UR agency. Hospitalization required UR approval. Surgery required UR approval. Extending the hospital stay for additional tests required UR approval. Transferring the patient to a rehabilitation center required UR approval.

At the same time as the U.S. government was establishing goals for utilization, it was promoting research to establish norms for care. The federal Agency for Health Care Policy Research was a major catalyst in this movement. Starting in the 1980s, the agency funded patient outcome research teams (PORTs) to review the available CEA evidence and recommend treatment norms for dozens of diseases. PROs used PORTS results to refine their oversight of Medicare. By the late 1980s, the PROs were selling their guidelines to private insurers and providers, under the name of *disease management*. Disease management provides norms for care based on the best available clinical evidence and goes a long way toward rationalizing medical decision-making. In the 1990s, providers, drugmakers, and consulting firms all joined the disease management bandwagon.

In many respects, UR and disease management attempt to do in the private sector what the Oregon Health Services Commission, NICE, PBAC, and other agencies are doing in the public sector. Ideally, the goal of a UR service agency is to weed out inefficient services. If cost-cutting is done correctly, the money saved can be used to hold down premiums, which in turn could result in expanded coverage or simply more money to spend on other things.

The critical question, then, is whether UR is done correctly. Needless to say, most MCOs believe that UR is worthwhile, while most physicians disagree. At the heart of this disagreement are two irresolvable conflicts. The first conflict stems from the different information available to UR agencies and physicians. UR agencies have access to the vast CEA literature, allowing them to identify the latest norms for care. These norms represent the proper course of treatment for the average patient. But physicians have information about the subtle aspects of their patients' health—their detailed medical histories, tolerance for pain, family support, and so forth. These idiosyncratic differences are critical to making the right prescription. To a certain extent, the debate between MCOs and physicians comes down to a simple question: Which information is more important? If adhering to the norms is more important than accounting for idiosyncrasies, then UR agencies should have the upper hand. Otherwise, physician autonomy is essential.

Taken in this light, the current system may not be so bad. Physicians who are unable to defend their recommendations may back off when a UR agency objects or when their recommendations deviate from established guidelines. But many other physicians will take the time necessary to explain why a patient differs from the norm. As a result, this system seems to respect both norms and idiosyncrasies. As CEA methods continue to improve, UR agencies will be able to refine their methods and account for more and more subtle differences across patients.

The second conflict stems from the profit motive. UR agencies make money by eliminating unnecessary services. Under fee-for-service medicine, physicians make money by providing more services. Naturally, UR agencies believe that physicians ignore costs, while physicians accuse UR agencies of hewing to the bottom line. Physicians are especially upset about having to practically beg to obtain some treatments, particularly if they have to negotiate with UR nurses rather than with other physicians. The resulting hostility cannot be overstated. Physicians are the leading supporters of patients' bill of rights laws that would eviscerate UR by sharply restricting payers' ability to deny reimbursement. But this legislation has been held up for several years, due in part to strenuous opposition by MCOs.

In the meantime, UR has undergone rapid change in the marketplace. During the 1990s, physicians and MCOs came to view UR as a costly game. MCOs paid UR agencies as much as 2 percent of total medical expenses for their services, yet had little to show in terms of cost reductions. One reason UR agencies had such a hard time reducing costs is that physicians learned that if they lobbied long and hard, they could always get what they wanted. By the late 1990s, MCOs were approving 99 percent of physician requests, and some payers began to wonder why they bothered with the process at all. In November 1999, United Healthcare dropped its UR requirement. Physicians hailed the apparent restoration of their autonomy. So did United Healthcare. Senior executives at United stated that medical decisions should be left to members and their physicians."[9] Other MCOs are watching and waiting to see if they will follow United Healthcare's lead.

Selective Contracting. The early prepaid groups were picky about choosing their members. They made sure that their physicians had the proper training and credentials. But they also wanted physicians who had conservative treatment styles and who would hold down costs. By the 1980s, insurers learned that selectively contracting with only a subset of all providers offered another way to reduce costs. MCOs secured deep discounts from providers by threatening to exclude them from their networks. To further enhance their bargaining power, some MCOs acted as if all providers were interchangeable, effectively commoditizing them.

Patients certainly do not believe that physicians are commodities. By the late 1990s, patients were demanding that MCOs expand their provider networks. Locked in fiercely competitive battles for employer contracts, MCOs obliged. Providers responded by raising their prices. For the time being, it appears that patients are willing to pay more to have access to their favorite providers.

Formularies. It stands to reason that the principles of selective contracting could apply to other medical services besides physicians and hospitals. In the late 1980s, a few independent companies such as Express Scripts, Value Rx, Medco, and Diversified Pharmacy Services began to selectively contract for prescription drugs. These pharmacy benefits management firms (PBMs), working on behalf of MCOs, assemble lists of approved drugs, also known as formularies. MCO enrollees who use drugs on the formularies pay at most a small copayment, perhaps $5 or $10. Enrollees using drugs that are off the formulary would have to pay as much as $50. PBMs provide pharmacists and physicians with computer software and, occasionally, financial incentives to further promote use of formulary drugs.

PBMs are the U.S. equivalent of national drug boards, and the formulary system has much in common with reference pricing. By setting the out-of-pocket prices for drugs, PBMs have the power to move market shares. They use that power to obtain deep discounts from drugmakers, and most of the savings are passed along to employers and employees. PBMs may occasionally exclude a drug altogether, thereby forcing patients to pay the full purchase price. This action can profoundly affect sales of that drug and may therefore enable PBMs to secure discounts that rival those obtained by national drug boards. By the mid-1990s, PBMs controlled access to prescription drugs for virtually every privately insured American.

Drugs that do not make it onto formularies are often prohibitively expensive, causing patients to select other drugs or go without any drug treatment. For example, in the wake of sharply curtailed federal payments to Medicare HMOs, most plans have dropped expensive drugs from their formularies.[10] Some of the affected drugs treat diseases such as AIDS, Alzheimer's, breast cancer, and prostate cancer. The costs of these drugs can be staggering, especially to seniors and the disabled, who had previously paid minimal or no copayments. Kaiser plans in California dropped coverage for Copaxone, an MS treatment that competes with beta-interferon. Seniors enrolled in Kaiser (and other health plans that have also dropped Copaxone) must now pay nearly $1,000 per month out of their own pockets for the injectable drug. Secure Horizons, a Texas HMO, stopped paying for certain types of chemotherapy. Patients were soon hit with $1,000 *weekly* bills.

Few private sector MCOs will completely exclude drugs from their formularies. More typically, they use "tiered formularies" in which copayments vary by tier. Thus, patients may pay $5 for a generic drug, $20 for a therapeutically equivalent branded drug, and $50 for the very latest and most expensive drug. The copayments are set so as to encourage patients to use the less costly drugs. The MCOs rely on the copayments to steer patients to the cheaper drugs. Such price rationing was relatively ineffective through much of the 1990s, and copayments increased to their current levels as a result.

PBM decision-making is a mix of hard-nosed price negotiations and scientifically driven cost-effectiveness analysis. When selecting among close substitutes, such as the anti-infective drugs Biaxin and Zithromax or the heart drugs Calan and Isoptin, PBMs are able to play one drugmaker off against another to obtain discounts of as much as 90 percent off the retail price. This strategy results in rationing, in the sense that most patients will end up using the drug chosen by the PBM, but it has little consequence for quality of care, inasmuch as the drugs are virtually identical.

When an expensive drug such as Viagra, the prostate drug Proscar, or the arthritis drug Celebrex has no close substitutes, PBMs review the cost-effectiveness literature to determine whether the benefits justify the cost. As in Europe and Canada, MCOs will pay more if they think the drug is worth it. But if the drug is of questionable value, PBMs may refuse to add it to the formulary or will require patients to make a large copayment. Then, price rationing kicks in.

Drugmakers use two strategies to improve the chances that their drugs will end up in favorable tiers on formularies, without having to give deep discounts. The first is to provide economic evidence to support the proposed prices. Drugmakers try to convince PBMs and MCOs that the cost per QALY for their drugs is in line with that for other drugs on the formulary. This is especially important for novel drugs for which it is difficult to establish a reference price. Thus far, PBMs and MCOs take the cost-per-QALY information into account when setting their formularies, but it is just one of many factors that they consider. Public perceptions about the value of drugs, relations with drug-makers, and a host of institutional factors can all outweigh cost-effectiveness.

DTC Advertising. The second strategy drugmakers use to win formulary approval is to bypass PBMs and market directly to patients through direct-to-consumer (DTC) advertising. Federal restrictions on DTC advertising of prescription drugs were relaxed in 1997. Prior to that, DTC ads mentioning drugs by name were required to detail the drugs' adverse effects, detracting from the advertising message. But the new law allowed drugmakers to market their products much like any other consumer goods, with only minimal mention of side effects. Drugmakers immediately launched multimillion-dollar DTC ad campaigns. Total DTC spending shot up from $800 million in 1996 to $2.5 billion in 2000, and it continues to grow.[11]

DTC ads have helped drugmakers overcome payer resistance to high prices of novel drugs. For example, many insurers were reluctant to pay for Viagra. One major payer, the Kaiser plans in California, claimed that the benefits were not worth the estimated $100 million annual cost.[12] Not only did Kaiser reckon that the use of Viagra was hardly a matter of life and death; it also anticipated moral hazard–induced utilization. But Pfizer launched a massive publicity campaign to boost demand for the drug and even lobbied state legislatures to compel HMOs to pay for it. Most HMOs gave in to public pressure. Kaiser held out. In 1998, an enrollee sued Kaiser to obtain coverage. Though the plaintiff won a lower court verdict, Kaiser prevailed on appeal.

Drugmakers especially rely on DTC ads when a product faces competition from a close substitute—think of Allegra and Claritin (for allergies) or Zocor and Lipitor (for high cholesterol). In the past, PBMs have treated these products as interchangeable and obtained large price concessions in exchange for exclusive formulary status. To make matters worse for the drugmakers, the rapid diffusion of scientific knowledge has made such competitive scenarios the norm. Prozac faces competition from Paxil, Zoloft, and Effexor. Prilosec (for ulcers) competes with Prevacid. Drugmakers try to win over PBMs through extensive sales efforts, but these have had only limited success. In the last few years, drugmakers have found a new way to differentiate their products in the eyes of American consumers by employing DTC advertising.

DTC appears to be working. HMOs are losing their leverage over drugs that have good substitutes. Many patients insist that their physicians write prescriptions for advertised drugs, even when a drug is off the formulary and an equally effective drug is on the formulary. As a result, PBMs are much less effective at moving market share, so drugmakers do not have to offer deep discounts. Moreover, many patients become upset to learn that their PBM formulary does not cover their favorite advertised drug, and they complain to their employers. Employers have reacted by favoring more generous PBM formularies, further enabling drugmakers to raise prices.

If PBMs lead to rationing by steering patients toward discounted drugs, then DTC is just another form of rationing, inasmuch as it steers patients toward heavily advertised drugs. It is informative to look at the content of DTC ads. Advocates of rational rationing might hope that DTC ads would tout the efficacy of the drugs, with claims like "Our drug offers a 10 percent better chance of recovery." They would be disappointed. DTC ads feature the usual Madison Avenue fare—testimonials from celebrities, scenes of happy children at play, and other image-related content. For now, at least, drugmakers do not believe they can sell the American public on superior outcomes. Better to sell their drugs on sizzle.

WHITHER RATIONING IN AMERICA?

Although there has always been rationing in America, it is rarely mentioned unless in a discussion of the uninsured. Insured Americans continue to enjoy greater access to care than just about anyone else in the world. But this situation may soon change. For the first time in a decade, Americans are expressing concern about rising health care costs. Health care spending has increased by nearly 10 percent in each of the last three years, and there is a lot of finger pointing. Selective contracting and prepayment have provided some savings but can do little to stop rising costs associated with new drugs and new medical technologies. So payers are pointing their fingers toward the pharmaceutical industry, and for good reason. Drug costs are rising by 15 percent annually, and in some plans the increase exceeds 20 percent. Other technology costs are rising as well. Expenditures for the latest scanners, laproscopic surgery, cardiac catheterization, hip prostheses, and countless other state-of-the-art medical services seem to be spiraling out of control.

ENOUGH IS ENOUGH

Payers are under enormous pressure to do something about costs. In the late 1990s I attended a presentation by Jim Mortimer, president of the Midwest Business Group on Health, a coalition of large employers concerned about health care costs. Someone in the audience asked Mr. Mortimer if Americans were better off with 1990s technology at 1990s costs or 1980s technology at 1980s costs. He immediately responded that we were better off in the 1980s. To his mind, the newest medical technology is not worth the cost. He claimed that most of the members of his coalition felt the same way. When it came to medical spending, enough was enough.

As individual patients, we will demand just about any medical service our physicians recommend, provided that someone else is paying for them. But if Mr. Mortimer is correct, those who foot the bill believe they can no longer afford to let patients (and their physicians) make their own decisions. Most developed nations have long since accepted the idea that it is appropriate for the government to ration access—that some treatments and technologies are not worth their cost. At some point, U.S. payers may draw a line in the sand as well.

This begs a question of fundamental importance: How does one determine whether medical services are worth their cost? The rest of this book is devoted to answering this question. Part of the answer lies in the science of CEA, which I describe in the next two chapters. Through CEA, it may be possible to rank health care interventions based on their bang for the buck and prioritize spending accordingly. England's NICE is an example of CEA in action. Oregon's Medicaid plan, profiled in Chapter 7, provides another example of the potential for CEA to save lives and money.

CEA may not be enough to satisfy Mr. Mortimer. Prioritizing health care spending is all well and good, but at some point, the American public must decide how much money to allocate toward medical services. To draw this line is to put a price on life itself. This may seem like an impossible task, but it is one that many people have to cope with every day. Government agencies deciding how much money to allocate to public health projects, juries awarding damages in wrongful death cases, employers paying workers to take on risky jobs, are all coming to terms with the price of life. Chapter 8 describes how to make such decisions, with a focus on methods that are gaining acceptance among economists. Not only do these methods suggest that Mr. Mortimer was terribly wrong about the value of new technology, but they also suggest that the kind of rationing done directly by Australia's PBS and England's NICE, and indirectly by other payers, may be penny-wise but pound-foolish.

ENDNOTES

1. K. Langa and E. Sussman, 1993, "The Effect of Cost-Containment Policies on Rates of Coronary Revascularization in California," *New England Journal of Medicine* 329 (24): 1784–89.

2. R. Pear, "Many Doctors Shun Patients with Medicare," *New York Times* 17 March 2002, sec. 1, p. 1.

3. A senior executive at the Kaiser HMO called the use of financial incentives the "reversal of economics." Quoted in C. Cutting,

1971, "Historical Development and Operating Concepts," in A. Somers, ed., *The Kaiser-Permanente Medical Program,* New York: Commonwealth Fund.

4. A. Enthoven, 1978, "Consumer-Choice Health Plan. Inflation and Inequity in Health Care Today: Alternatives for Cost Control and an Analysis of Proposals for National Health Insurance, Parts 1 and 2," *New England Journal of Medicine* 298(12): 650–59 and 298(13): 709–19.

5. A Nixon health care advisor learned about HMOs after sharing an airplane ride with Paul Ellwood.

6. H. Luft, 1978, "How Do Health Maintenance Organizations Achieve Their 'Savings'?" *New England Journal of Medicine* 298(24): 1336–43.

7. Perhaps the best paper documenting how incentives affect physician services is M. Gaynor and P. Gertler, 1995, "Moral Hazard and Risk Spreading in Partnerships," *RAND Journal of Economics* 26: 591–614.

8. W. Manning et al., 1984, "A Controlled Trial of the Effect of a Prepaid Group Practice on Use of Services," *New England Journal of Medicine* 310(23): 1505–10.

9. Quoted in S. Jordon, "Managed Care Makeover," *Omaha World Journal* 9 January 2000 p. 1R.

10. To be fair to the HMOs, the regular Medicare program has no prescription drug benefit at all.

11. *MedAd News,* February 2002, p. 1.

12. M. Vanzi, 1998, "State Investigates Kaiser's Refusal to Provide Viagra," *Los Angeles Times* 3 July 1998, p. A, p. 3.

5 DOING COST-EFFECTIVENESS AND COST-BENEFIT RESEARCH

The premise of health care rationing is that left to their own devices, patients and physicians will make poor health care decisions. Payers have tried several strategies to limit inefficiencies in the current system. U.S. indemnity insurers and the French (through their *ticket modérateur*) require patients to make hefty copayments. HMOs and the British health trusts capitate physicians. Nationalized health systems in Canada and England restrict the supply of specialists and sharply curtail expenditures on medical equipment, creating lengthy waiting lists.

These strategies have certainly reduced costs, but they are far from ideal. The drawback of waiting lists goes without saying. Small copayments are effective at eliminating unnecessary but relatively minor expenses. But they are less effective when it comes to major expenses. And insurers cannot reasonably ask patients to pay a substantial percentage of a high medical bill, since this would defeat the point of health insurance. Indeed, the French have repeatedly found that efforts to increase the *ticket modérateur* are unpopular and politically dangerous.[1] When the government did manage to push through increases, French citizens purchased complementary insurance to cover the copayment. Much the same occurred in the United States, in the late 1980s, when the federal government enacted a law that would provide prescription drug coverage for seniors, but only with substantial copayments. Loud protests led to a hasty repeal, and the law never took effect. In any realistic insurance plan, it seems that price rationing will play only a limited role.

Changing physician incentives also has limitations. Thanks to Kaiser's "reversal of economics," Kaiser physicians provide fewer services than do their fee-for-service counterparts. Many HMOs go Kaiser one step further, penalizing physicians whose patients utilize a lot of services. Such payment schemes put physicians in the unenviable position of having to choose between their own financial viability and their desire to deliver services to their patients. Much of the backlash against managed care comes from the tensions created by this unhealthy conflict of interest.

Perhaps the single biggest problem with most of these "solutions" is that they do not directly address the problems that everyone is bemoaning. National governments and U.S. employers may complain about rising spending, but that is not a valid concern. They have all increased spending in other areas, such as information technology, with few complaints. The problem is not increasing health care spending per se. The problem is that we spend our health care dollars inefficiently, due to moral hazard, demand inducement, and practice variations. Waiting lists and other solutions may reduce spending, but that is a feeble accomplishment. Any payer can cut back health care spending by simply refusing to open its wallet. But current strategies for reducing spending do not create a more efficient health care system, except by happenstance. If anything, the intrusion of politics into health care we have seen throughout the world suggests that these cost-containment solutions can make things worse.

Rational rationing through cost-effectiveness analysis (CEA) is the only cost-containment solution that explicitly promotes efficient medical decision-making. Rational rationing is at the heart of new programs such as England's NICE and Australia's PBS. But it is hardly a newfangled, untested approach. CEA has been a cornerstone of public policy for over a hundred years.[2]

SOME BACKGROUND ON CEA

In 1902, the U.S. Army Corps of Engineers used CEA to choose among several river and harbor projects. The Corps remains a major practitioner of CEA, recently using these methods to assess ways to ease flooding along the Mississippi River. Many other U.S. government agencies also use CEA. President Kennedy's Department of Defense used CEA to evaluate projects. In the 1980s, the U.S. Congress enacted legislation subjecting all government programs to CEA. In fact, CEA is used all around the world. The Japanese Environmental Ministry uses CEA to evaluate pollution abatement programs. The Mexican government is using CEA to help locate a new international airport for Mexico City.

In all these applications of CEA, government agencies have a limited amount of money and are looking for the best way to spend it. Just like health care payers, they want the biggest bang for their buck. The Army Corps of Engineers wanted the greatest protection of farmland per dollar. Kennedy's Department of Defense wanted the greatest protection of life and property per dollar. Japan's Environmental Ministry wants the greatest reduction in pollution per yen. Mexico wants the biggest growth in air travel per peso. Such approaches make so much sense that the public readily accepts the results.

IS IT VALID TO USE CEA FOR HEALTH CARE?

These traditional applications of CEA involve goods or services whose benefits are shared by many people at the same time. Economists call these *public goods*. (Goods and services whose benefits are not shared widely are called *private goods*.) It makes sense for government agencies to fret over how best to provide public goods such as flood control or the national defense, because otherwise they might not be provided at all. Even the staunchest libertarians grudgingly accept government involvement in the provision of public goods.

Virtually all health care services are private goods, however. In markets for private goods, government involvement is usually kept to a minimum. This makes sense too. After all, who needs the government dictating what clothes to wear or what food to eat? So, why should patients allow the government to decide what health care services they can and cannot obtain? One reason is that even though health care services are private goods, they are often paid for with public dollars. This means that if Peter undergoes treatment, there might not be enough money left over to treat Paul. Paul could always spend his own money for the treatment, but medical care can be very expensive and Paul might not be able to afford it. If funds are scarce, then Paul would certainly want the government to oversee Peter's treatment decision. So too might the taxpayers who have to pay for the treatment, regardless of who receives it.

It is doubtful that many people would want the government to intervene if Peter's treatment could save his life. But it would be a different matter if it turned out that Peter's treatment was frivolous or of little value. After all, if everyone received frivolous services, then the government would be unable to pay for truly valuable services without further tax increases. Only the wealthy would be able to obtain the costly medical services they really need, a situation that most people would find intolerable. For this reason, cash-starved health care systems have sought to make sure their money is wisely spent.

There is an analogy to be drawn between medical decision making and children buying toys. On their own, neither children nor physicians and their patients can be counted on to make the wisest decisions. Parents who want to get the most out of their family budget know that they must occasionally ration their children's toy purchases. To get the most out of their household budget, they will carefully weigh the benefits of a new toy against the price. It follows that a health care payer that wishes to get the most out of its budget should also try to balance benefits against costs.

CEA, and its cousin cost-benefit analysis (CBA), are central to this balancing act. CEA ranks alternative expenditures on the basis of "bang for the buck." CBA directly asks whether the bang is worth the buck. CBA/CEA methods form the foundation of rational rationing schemes in England, Australia, and Oregon. Advocates of these schemes take comfort in the scientific foundations and long history of CBA/CEA. Indeed, the medical research community has almost universally endorsed CBA/CEA as an appropriate guide to medical decision-making. But CBA/CEA is not an exact science, and there are some unresolved issues in how to conduct research and tabulate the results. Given the potential for error and, even worse, manipulation, one may wonder whether rational rationing will do more harm than good.

DOING CEA/CBA

At first blush, it seems to be a rather straightforward task to perform CEA/CBA analysis. One just needs measures of benefits and costs, and the rest is simple algebra. Needless to say, the devil is in the details. And what a lot of details there are!

Fortunately, researchers have reached a broad consensus about many key details of CEA/CBA analysis. For example, the first step in any CEA/CBA analysis is to select a point of view. Insured patients, who can disregard costs when seeking care, may see things one way. Providers, whose incomes depend on whether they perform the treatment, may see things another way. Insurers, who have to foot the bill but do not directly enjoy any of the benefits, may have an entirely different perspective. Most researchers have adopted the convention of taking society's point of view. This perspective tallies all the health benefits and nonhealth benefits (such as improved worker productivity) of treatment, regardless of who benefits, and weighs them against all the costs of care, regardless of who bears the burden.

There is also considerable agreement about the need for careful research design. If practical, medical researchers try to perform *randomized double-blind* studies, in which patients are randomly assigned to receive competing interventions or a placebo, and neither researchers nor patients know who has received which treatment. The randomized double-blind study is the gold standard for all CEA/CBA research because it eliminates many potential sources of research bias. Cohort studies, in which researchers follow a large group of study subjects for many years, are sometimes a good alternative to randomized studies. (Much of our knowledge about diet and prevention comes from cohort studies.) There are a variety of other study designs that may provide reliable data for CEA/CBA analysis. But no study design is perfect. Randomized trials may be free from bias, but they may not be useful for predicting what will happen to patients in less controlled settings. Research designs in real-world settings may be biased due to the lack of random assignment and the fact that providers and patients often know they are under observation.

Most managed care organizations and government regulators understand the limitations of different research designs, and they usually give little credence to research findings that have not been published in peer-reviewed academic journals. Not all peer-reviewed journals are created equal, however. A single study in the *New England Journal of Medicine* or *Lancet*, which have extremely high standards for validity, can be more persuasive than several contradictory studies in less highly regarded journals. Most impressive of all are meta-analyses, which combine results from the best of earlier studies. A meta-analysis in a top journal can immediately affect medical decision-making worldwide.

Yet there are many problems in relying totally on published studies. In the prestigious Shattuck Lecture to the Massachusetts Medical Society (publisher of the *New England Journal of Medicine*), Barbara McNeil identified several limitations of even the best published research.[3] One problem is that it often takes five years or longer from the start of a research trial until publication. This delay may retard acceptance of important new technologies, as was the case for the use of positron-emission tomography for diagnosing certain cancers. At the same time, new technologies may be perfected that render obsolete the results of recently published studies.

Such was the case for implantable defibrillators, which replaced certain forms of coronary bypass surgery just as research about the latter was published.

McNeil identified other problems. Studies with negative findings are disproportionately less likely to get published. A set of studies might disagree about the merits of an intervention, but only the positive results will see the light of day. Finally, study groups are often unrepresentative of the population as a whole, and it is often difficult to extrapolate the findings to other groups. Most studies do a fine job of measuring the effects of interventions on middle-aged white men, but researchers often fail to include sufficient numbers of women, blacks, and young and old patients.

McNeil did not mention one other area of concern. Despite the best efforts of journal editors and reviewers, many researchers have overlooked the important and related issues of how to measure costs and how much weight to put on future costs and benefits.

MEASURING COSTS

Analysts agree on the basic methods for measuring costs. At first blush, this does not seem surprising. Ask someone how much a new pair of shoes cost, and he or she can easily tell you the price. Now ask someone who just had an MRI how much that cost. Once again, the person can probably tell you how much he or she paid. Therein lies the problem. A patient who is fully insured might tell you that the MRI did not cost anything. But someone had to pay for the MRI, and the societal perspective must account for the expense. Thus, researchers must measure the cost of providing services rather than the amount paid to receive them.

Measuring provider costs is a simple concept, but is surprisingly difficult in practice. Cost accounting in most medical care organizations ranges from poor to nonexistent. One reason is that accountants have a difficult time figuring out how to allocate substantial overhead costs such as the administration expenses and the cost of medical equipment. But there are a host of other technical issues that accountants have yet to resolve. Some providers, including many physician practices, do not even have accounting data.

As a result of these accounting problems, efforts to measure costs often boil down to educated guesswork. For example, my own research found that the accounting costs of ventilator therapy for crippled children vastly overstated the actual costs. Remember that the access of crippled children to ventilator therapy may depend entirely on costs—so we need to know whether the accounting is done correctly. Other research suggests that the costs of emergency room care have been wildly overstated, and the costs of some outpatient services have been overstated. Unfortunately, such biases remain commonplace throughout the CEA/CBA literature.

If possible, researchers should also account for *indirect costs* of medical care, which include the value of any time lost from work, as well as other inconveniences. For some treatments, the indirect costs may be just as important as direct costs. The U.S. National Institutes of Health reports that the indirect costs of diseases such as diabetes and asthma may exceed the direct medical costs. This fact makes it essential for researchers to account for indirect costs when studying treatments for these diseases. For example, a study of an asthma drug that fails to account for indirect costs may grossly understate the benefit/cost ratio. As a result, the drug may fail to pass muster in a rational rationing plan.

Things get even messier once we take the long view. It stands to reason that treatments today can affect costs in the future. Beta-blocker therapy can prevent future heart attacks. Smoking cessation programs can prevent future lung cancers. To provide a fair assessment of the costs of these interventions, it is necessary to subtract the anticipated future savings from the total costs. This is common practice in CBA/CEA research and explains why preventive interventions such as prenatal care and colon cancer screening are among the most cost-effective of all health care interventions.

There is unanimous agreement among researchers to give credit to interventions that reduce future costs. But some interventions can lead to higher costs in the future. Consider the case of an elderly woman who undergoes hip replacement surgery. The cost of treatment should certainly include the cost of her hospital stay. But what if she requires additional medical care after discharge, perhaps home nursing or physical therapy? It makes sense to include these costs as well, and most research studies do.

So far, so good: Researchers agree to include all future medical costs, whether on the upside or downside. Suppose that the woman with the new hip becomes more active. As a result, she has a heart attack and needs costly medical therapy. Many researchers argue that the cost of the therapy should be included in the cost of the hip replacement. After all, the woman would not have needed the therapy had she not received the new hip. There is some logic to this argument, especially if the researcher can show that the hip replacement increased the chances of the heart attack. Most researchers agree that future medical costs should be part of the CBA/CEA equation, provided they are directly tied to the intervention in question.

There is some question as to how far to push this logic. Suppose that the newly active woman starts driving again, gets into an accident, and totals her car. Should we add the cost of a new car to the cost of the surgery? Even if the woman remains healthy for years to come, she will spend money on food and housing, and perhaps even a few extravagances. Should we include these costs as well?

Strange as it seems, some researchers believe that CBA/CEA studies should include all future nonmedical costs.[4] They argue that if an intervention causes a patient to live longer or to change his or her lifestyle, then the resulting costs are directly attributable to the intervention and should count against it. Including all future costs can greatly alter CEA/CBA measures by favoring quality-of-life interventions over life-extending interventions. (The latter tend to drive up future costs more than the former). Chemotherapy fares particularly badly; one study shows that the cost-effectiveness of some forms of chemotherapy falls by half or more when future costs are accounted for.[5] Payers who are willing to cover chemotherapy may reconsider their decision if future costs are included in the analysis.

Although the technical analysis supporting this argument appears to be correct, the implication is disquieting, as it portrays the expenses of the elderly as a drain on society's resources. It is no wonder that a 1996 U.S. Public Health Service Panel failed to reach a consensus on the issue and left the decision to account for future costs up to individual practitioners.

DISCOUNTING

When given a choice between paying for something now or paying later, most people prefer to pay later, as long as they do not have to pay a substantial interest charge. The same logic applies to medical costs, and researchers usually give less weight to future costs than to current costs. Researchers reduce future costs by the discount rate, which is the interest rate that leaves individuals indifferent between paying now or paying later. If you are indifferent between spending $5,000 on a big-screen television today or making a deferred payment of $5,250 in one year, then your discount rate is about 5 percent.

It seems reasonable for researchers to discount future health care costs. But this idea raises a fascinating question. Should researchers also discount future benefits? This is the same as asking whether a year of life in the future is worth less than a year of life today. It is important to answer this question because many interventions require us to spend money today to enjoy health benefits in the future. If we discount the value of future years of life, then many treatments, especially preventive treatments, might not seem worth the cost.

To many people, the answer to the question seems obvious. A life is a life, no matter when it is lived, so it is ridiculous to discount future lives. What is obvious may also be wrong. The argument in favor of discounting future life-years is both ingenious and compelling. The key to the argument is to show that failure to discount leads to an absurd conclusion. This forces us to accept the premise that lives today are worth more than lives in the future.

The argument in favor of discounting relies on two assumptions that seem very reasonable. The first is that there are always likely to be some individuals who go without needed medical services. The second is that it is possible to invest money today and receive a return that exceeds the rate of inflation. If these assumptions are valid, then we could divert money that we currently spend on health care and invest it instead. The resulting sum, multiplied through investments, permits even more health care spending in the future. So, eliminating current health care spending and investing the money will lead to more life-years saved in the future.

If we really believe that future lives are worth just as much as current lives, then the only logical thing to do is to sharply curtail current health care spending. Although this will cause the loss of many life-years, by saving the money and spending it in the future, we can save even more life-years. But this is absurd. Few people would seriously propose letting large numbers of people die today because our money can save more lives in the future. We are forced to conclude that future lives are worth less than current lives!

All researchers agree about the need to discount future lives. But there is considerable disagreement about exactly what discount rate to use. It turns out that small differences in discount rates can have a big impact on CEA/CBA findings. Suppose we are evaluating a cancer prevention program that will save 1,000 life-years 20 years from now. If we use a discount rate of 2 percent, those 1,000 life-years are "worth" 668 life-years today. But if we increase the discount rate to 6 percent, they are worth only 290 life-years. The reported cost-effectiveness of the prevention program would fall by more than half. The choice of discount rate could make or break funding for the program. Most researchers use a discount rate of about 5 percent, which is consistent with the rate at which costs are usually discounted.

IS CEA/CBA RESEARCH VALID?

Patients will not embrace rational rationing if they do not believe that the underlying science is valid. Despite a broad consensus on how to perform most aspects of CBA/CEA analysis, there appear to be ample opportunities for mistakes and biases to creep in. The few examples cited above suggest that funding for treatments and programs such as ventilator therapy, chemotherapy, and cancer prevention may depend on choice of research methods.

It should be no surprise, then, that different researchers may reach different conclusions about the cost-effectiveness of particular interventions. When the intervention affects millions of people and the findings are highly publicized, confusion can result. Such has been the case for annual and biennial mammograms for women age 40 to 49. A series of articles published in leading medical journals in the mid- to late 1990s reported costs per life-year saved ranging from under $10,000 to over $100,000. One might think that these studies examined different populations, but most of these studies use data from the same sample of Swedish women. Results differ for a variety of reasons. For example, the benefits of breast cancer screening in women age 40 to 49 may not be realized for more than 10 years, so the studies are particularly sensitive to the choice of discount rate. Because the findings have been so inconsistent, there have been a series of ambiguous recommendations about whether women in this age group should receive annual, biennial, or any screening at all.

The U.S. National Cancer Institute currently recommends either annual or biennial screening. Meanwhile, some evidence from an older Canadian study questions the need for mammograms more than once every 5 years. This research has prompted investigators in the United States and elsewhere to ask the Swedish scientists to provide access to their data. Some researchers, who believe that the Swedes used faulty methods, want to conduct independent analyses.

Payers understand that CBA/CEA analyses are two parts science and one part art, and they are skeptical of studies that purport to show that expensive new treatments are cost-effective. To win over payers, drug companies try to publish their findings. But payers are suspicious of even published, peer-reviewed industry-sponsored research, perhaps with good reason. Pharmaceutical industry–sponsored studies report benefit/cost ratios that are, on average, three times higher than the benefit/cost ratios reported in government-sponsored studies.[6]

To restore confidence in their work, pharmaceutical companies are hoping to establish standards for cost-effectiveness research. The International Society of Pharmacoeconomics and Outcomes Research has 2,000 members drawn from academia and industry. The society has created several task forces charged with establishing best practices in CEA research. Companies that adhere to these standards should find payers far more receptive to their findings.

CBA/CEA IN PRACTICE

Despite payer skepticism, CBA/CEA studies do matter. One of the great success stories of the biotech revolution, Genentech, owes much to the power of CBA/CEA. Among biotech companies, Genentech is second only to Amgen in worldwide revenues. Genentech was founded in 1976, and during its first decade, the company established a solid reputation based on scientific advancement rather than actual products. In 1987, the company introduced one of its first breakthrough treatments, tissue plasminogen activator (tPA) a thrombolytic anticlotting agent. Physicians prescribe thrombolytic agents to patients who are suspected of having had a heart attack. Prior to the introduction of tPA, the agent of choice was streptokinase. The price of a dose of streptokinase was $200. Genentech boldly set the price of tPA at $2,200 per dose, claiming a scientific advantage for the new product.

The company promoted the theoretical benefits of tPA over streptokinase, but there were as yet no studies directly comparing the two treatments. Even so, Genentech forecast that tPA would quickly replace streptokinase as the thrombolytic agent of choice. Wall Street's enthusiasm for biotech contributed to the hype about the product. Genentech was so certain of tPA's success that the company worried about having shortages. But doctors proved reluctant to prescribe tPA, leaving Genentech with a surplus that forced it to shut down production in mid-1988 and take a reserve against earnings. As of 1990, most U.S. insurers had reluctantly agreed to pay for tPA, which barely surpassed streptokinase in the U.S. market. Many national health systems still refused to pay for tPA, however, preferring to wait for the results of research studies.

Several clinical trials were under way. In these trials, patients who had a heart attack were randomly assigned to receive either streptokinase or tPA. Researchers monitored the patients for up to six months to determine which drug had a lower mortality rate. Researchers did not give much consideration to other benefits, such as improved functional status or reductions in future medical costs.

The results of initial studies published in 1991 and 1992 did not favor Genentech. At least two studies found no statistically significant difference in mortality rates. Armed with this evidence, payers pressured Genentech to reduce the price of tPA, and Genentech's revenues from tPA fell by 15 percent. But in 1993, researchers published results from the Global Utilization of Streptokinase and Tissue Plasminogen Activator for Occluded Coronary Arteries trial, better known as GUSTO. The study, which was sponsored by Genentech and appeared in the *New England Journal of Medicine*, involved 15 nations and 41,000 patients. The study was so big that it was dubbed a "mega-trial." Due to its sheer size and scope, the GUSTO findings took precedence over the results from earlier, smaller trials. The GUSTO results were good news for Genentech. GUSTO found that the mortality rate for patients who received tPA was 6 percent. The death rate for patients who received streptokinase was 7 percent. The difference of 1 percentage point was statistically significant.

Genentech had cleared an important hurdle. The best available evidence showed that tPA was medically effective, giving patients a 14 percent better chance of surviving. (One in seven patients who would have died would survive because of the new tPA treatment.) It was true that Genentech had paid $55 million for the GUSTO study, but the research design ensured that there was little possibility of bias, and the study was published in a prestigious journal.

Genentech's next step was to show that tPA was cost-effective. Fortunately for Genentech, the trade-off between dollars and lives could not be more explicit. Treating 100 patients with tPA instead of streptokinase would cost an extra $200,000 and would, on average, save one life. It was up to payers to decide whether this benefit justified the expense.

Genentech made the following case for tPA. At that time, a heart attack survivor could be expected to live for an additional 6 years. At a cost of $200,000 per life saved, the cost-effectiveness ratio works out to $33,333 per life-year. This was very much in line with the $20,000 to $60,000 per life-year that payers in Canada and Europe were routinely spending for other interventions. The price of tPA may have been high, but the benefits justified the cost. The argument was compelling, most payers agreed to cover tPA, and tPA regained all of its lost sales and more.

Genentech's efforts to promote tPA through CBA/CEA analysis were simplified by the focus on mortality. The principal benefit of tPA is that it saves lives, and it does so at a fairly reasonable cost. But many interventions improve the quality of life. Some highly cost-effective interventions, such as routine dental flossing, only affect the quality of life. This fact complicates CBA/CEA. It is one thing to say that tPA costs $33,333 per life-year saved and compare this figure against the cost-effectiveness of other lifesaving interventions. But how does one compare the benefits of cataract surgery to improve vision against the benefits of a hip replacement to help someone walk? And is it possible to compare these improvements in the quality of life against the costs? Researchers must answer these questions if they are to perform CEA/CBA on life-enhancing interventions. Chapter 6 describes how researchers are making quantitative comparisons of the value of vision, walking, and hundreds of other aspects of our health.

ENDNOTES

1. For more on the French efforts to raise copayments, see S. Sandier and P. Lancry, 1999, "Rationing Health Care in France" *Health Policy* 50: 23–38.

2. This brief history of CEA is taken from K. Warner and B. Luce, 1992, "Cost-Benefit and Cost-Effectiveness Analysis in Health Care," Ann Arbor, MI: Health Administration Press.

3. For further discussion of these issues and examples, see B. McNeil, 2001, "Hidden Barriers to Improvement in the Quality of Care," *New England Journal of Medicine* 345(22): 1612–20.

4. See D. Meltzer, 1997, "Accounting for Future Costs in Medical Cost-Effectiveness Analysis," *Journal of Health Economics* 16(1): 33–64.

5. Meltzer, D., ibid.

6. P. Neumann et al., 2000, "Are Pharmaceuticals Cost-Effective? A Review of the Evidence," *Health Affairs* 19(2): 92–109. Note that the bias could come from either the choice of methods or the choice of drugs studied.

6 MEASURING THE QUALITY OF LIFE

A friend of mine was recently diagnosed with prostate cancer. Fortunately, the tumor was still small and treatable. A surgeon removed his prostate, and my friend has enjoyed a complete recovery. This comes at a time when there is ongoing debate about how to diagnose prostate cancer, especially for older men who are at risk for the condition but may have no symptoms. The dreaded digital rectal exam (DRE) is the standard diagnostic tool for asymptomatic patients. However, the DRE can miss very small tumors. Many physicians prefer the prostate-specific antigen (PSA) test, which can catch some tumors missed by the DRE.

Unfortunately, the PSA test is not always accurate. About 5 percent of healthy patients will have a false-positive test result. Patients who receive false-positive test results may needlessly undergo costly interventions such as biopsies or surgery. While these interventions do not usually pose a risk of death, they can cause complications that reduce the quality of life; some patients may become incontinent or impotent.

This problem creates a thorny dilemma for researchers trying to document the cost-effectiveness of the PSA test. Research shows that the PSA test saves lives. One study reports a cost per life-year saved of about $16,000, which is below the typical threshold used to draw the line on cost-effectiveness.[1] However, a full evaluation of the PSA test should also account for any unwelcome complications. Once that is done, researchers will need to compare the benefits of life-years saved against the cost of complications. Therein lies the problem: How does one compare life-years saved against other health outcomes, such as impotence? To do this, researchers must have a common yardstick to measure all the possible health outcomes of the PSA test.

Health services researchers call such a yardstick a *rating scale*. Rating scales give a numerical score to life, death, and all medical conditions in between, including incontinence and impotence. Researchers have staked the future of CBA/CEA on their ability to construct valid rating scales. Without the scales, it would be impossible to fully evaluate most interventions.

Rating scales have been around for 30 years, beginning with the pioneering work of George Torrance.[2] In constructing these scales, researchers have surveyed thousands of people about whether they would prefer to be impotent or incontinent, hearing impaired or vision impaired, dizzy or nauseated. More importantly, they have quantified the responses. Thus, rating scales not only tell us whether being incontinent is worse than being impotent but whether it is 10 percent worse or 50 percent worse. This comparison, in turn, enables researchers to directly compare the cost-effectiveness of different interventions, even when they lead to seemingly non-comparable medical outcomes.

USING RATING SCALES TO MEASURE HEALTH STATES

Researchers have developed more than a half dozen different types of rating scales. Some of the best-known scales measure Healthy Year Equivalents (HYEs), Disability-Adjusted Life-Years (DALYs), and Quality-Adjusted Life-Years (QALYs). The scales have many features in common. The QALY scale, the most popular, is the basis for NICE's rationing program. I will use it as an example of how all the scales work.

The QALY scale provides a numerical score for different states of health, or what researchers call *health states*. Examples of health states are "dead," "completely healthy," and "complete visual impairment" (i.e., blind). Health states may include multiple conditions, such as "visual impairment and needs a wheelchair." They may be broad (e.g., "needs assistance walking") or narrow (e.g., "occasionally needs assistance climbing stairs"). Narrow health states are particularly helpful for evaluating interventions that have subtle health benefits.

A year of full health is worth 1 QALY. Death is worth 0 QALYs. Depending on how individuals respond to survey questions, a year of blindness might score 0.5 QALYs and a year of incontinence might score 0.75 QALYs. It is conceivable that some health states, such as quadriplegia, might score less than 0 QALYs. This would mean that people would rather be dead than quadriplegic. Table 6.1 gives an example of published QALY scores.[3]

TABLE 6.1   Some QALY scores. Reprinted with the permission of Cambridge University Press.

HEALTH STATE	QALY SCORE
Full health	1.00
Tired and sleepless	0.82
Frequent vomiting	0.55
Visual impairment and limited activities	0.50
Needs wheelchair	0.37
Dead	0.00

WORKING WITH QALYS

QALY scores can be manipulated mathematically. They can be added: If one year of blindness scores 0.5 QALYs, then four years of blindness would score 2 QALYs. Similarly, if two blind individuals each live one year, they have a total of 1 QALY. QALYs can also be multiplied: An intervention that offers a blind person a 50 percent chance of fully recovering her eyesight (QALY = 1) and a 50 percent chance of no improvement in vision (QALY = 0.5) has a QALY score of 0.75.[4]

Researchers can use QALYs to compute cost-effectiveness scores for treating different health states. Before seeing how this is done, it is useful to attempt a CEA without QALY scores. Suppose you wanted to compare two hypothetical treatments, one for incontinence and one for impotence. Table 6.2 gives some information about the interventions.[5]

TABLE 6.2   Comparison of Treatments for Incontinence and Impotence

CONDITION	COST OF TREATMENT	YEARS OF EFFECTIVENESS
Incontinence	$20,000	8
Impotence	$18,000	12

The data in Table 6.2 reveal that the treatment for incontinence is more expensive than the treatment for impotence and does not last as long. Unfortunately, there is no way to decide whether this fact makes the incontinence treatment more or less cost-effective than the impotence treatment. To do that, we need to know which is worse—incontinence or impotence—and by how much. Without QALY scores, this would necessarily be an apples-to-oranges comparison, and we could not get a valid answer. Instead, suppose that we have QALY scores shown in Table 6.3 for each condition.

TABLE 6.3   Comparison of Treatments with QALY Scores

CONDITION	QALY SCORE	COST OF TREATMENT	YEARS OF EFFECTIVENESS
Incontinence	.75	$20,000	8
Impotence	.9	$18,000	12

Armed with the QALY scores in Table 6.3, we can compare the cost-effectiveness of each treatment. First we compute the cost-effectiveness of the incontinence treatment. Someone who is successfully treated for incontinence gains 0.25 QALYs for each year that the treatment is effective.

(This is because the QALY score increases from 0.75 to 1.) Over 8 years, this adds up to 2 QALYs (ignoring discounting). In other words, the treatment provides a gain of 2 QALYs per patient. At $20,000 per treatment, the cost-effectiveness ratio is $10,000 per QALY gained.

Curing impotence generates a gain of 0.1 QALYs per year. (The QALY score increases from 0.9 to 1.) Over 12 years, this adds up to 1.2 QALYS. At a cost of $18,000, we spend $15,000 per QALY gained.[6] We conclude that the treatment for incontinence has a lower cost per QALY and is therefore more cost-effective.

Using methods like these, researchers have ranked the cost-effectiveness of thousands of interventions. They call these rankings *league tables*, like the rankings of teams in sports leagues. Table 6.4 shows excerpts drawn from two recently published league tables.[7]

TABLE 6.4   A League Table

INTERVENTION	COST PER QALY GAINED (1998 DOLLARS)
Hip replacement	$2,000
Kidney transplant	$7,500
Captopril therapy for 60-year-old patient surviving a heart attack	$11,000
Hospital hemodialysis	$35,000
Erythropoieten treatment for anemia in dialysis patients	$86,000
Open cholecystectomy vs. lithotripsy for treatment of gallstones	$140,000
Neurosurgery for malignant intracranial tumors	$320,000
Bone marrow transplant for younger patients with intermediate- or late-stage non-Hodgkin's lymphoma	Cost-increasing and QALY-reducing

Hip replacement surgery is in first place in Table 6.4. If the objective is to maximize QALYs with a fixed-budget constraint, then money should be allocated to provide all necessary hip replacements. Neurosurgery for malignant intracranial tumors is in next-to-last place. This procedure should be performed only if there is enough money to perform all the procedures ranked above it. Bone marrow transplant for younger patients with intermediate- or late-stage non-Hodgkin's lymphoma should never be funded—it increases costs and decreases quality of life.

PUTTING QALYS INTO PRACTICE

League tables allow policymakers to easily compare many interventions at once. This analysis, in turn, allows them to determine how best to spend scarce health care dollars. Policymakers can even rank new treatments alongside existing ones and then approve those with high rankings. As you will see in Chapter 7, regulators in Oregon have already put these ideas into practice for the state's Medicaid program. Unfortunately, the simplicity of this method is deceptive. The QALY approach raises a host of methodological and ethical issues. The future of rational rationing seems to be inextricably linked to QALYs, so it is essential to explore these issues in depth.

ALL QALYS ARE EQUAL

To compute QALYs and construct league tables, researchers treat all QALYs equally. If you have the same health state as someone else, you receive the same QALY score. Moreover, your QALYs are no more or less important than anyone else's. Rich or poor, black or white, male or female, young or old, each person's QALY counts the same. The "all QALYs are equal" (AQAE) assumption makes it easy to take the societal viewpoint. To compute the overall well-being of society, just add up everyone's QALYs.

The AQAE assumption justifies the mathematical manipulations of QALYs. Discounting aside, AQAE society does not care whether Jack lives 10 more years with a health state that scores 0.5 QALYs per year or Susan lives 5 more years at full health. Either way, society gets 5 more QALYs. Nor does society care whether 10 people each live 1 more year at full health or 1 person lives 10 more years. Either way, society gets 10 more QALYs. The bottom line to the AQAE society is the total number of QALYs it enjoys, no matter how they are divided among the population.

An important criticism of the AQAE assumption is that it ignores the obvious fact that individuals have widely diverging attitudes about health. Under AQAE, health states are ranked by consensus opinion, and health dollars allocated accordingly. This means that your access to treatment for a specific condition depends on what others think about that condition—your opinion does not count. You may dread the idea of having to walk with a limp. Nevertheless, if survey respondents give limping a high QALY score, then relatively little public money will go to preventing or treating your limp. If this approach were applied to ice cream, we might all have to eat vanilla. Preferences obviously vary from one person to the next, and a completely free market respects those differences. Despite this criticism, QALY supporters argue that simplicity and equity justify the AQAE assumption. Besides, if we drop AQAE, then we all have a selfish incentive to state that we dread the particular condition we happen to suffer from.

MEASURING QALYS

There are thousands of health states. (One study identified 900 health states just for neonates.) Each health state requires a QALY score. Each QALY score requires the opinions of hundreds of individuals. This means that hundreds of thousands of individuals have contributed their opinions to the construction of QALYs. Even so, most people have never heard of QALYs, and many who have heard of QALYs have no idea how they are measured.

Researchers measure QALY scores by asking carefully worded questions of a large cross-section of respondents. Respondents usually begin by reading a description of the condition in question, such as blindness. Most of us can imagine what it might be like to be blind, but the description of blindness might remind us of the various limitations that blindness would impose on our ability to work and function normally. Once respondents are familiar with the health states under consideration, researchers may choose from one of three approaches to ascertain the QALY scores.

The *relative scale approach* is by far the easiest. There are several ways to implement this approach. Here is one example you can try yourself.

CONSIDER THE FOLLOWING LINE THAT RANKS
HEALTH STATES ON A SCALE FROM 0 TO 1:

0	.25	.5	.75	1

Dead   Full health

Use a pencil to mark where you would place blindness on this line.

Once you have drawn your mark for blindness, it is very simple to compute the QALY score. If you put blindness in the very middle of the line, then you have implicitly given it a QALY score of 0.5. To be sure that you give useful responses, the researcher might remind you that if you placed blindness at 0.95, this would imply that you did not think it was much worse than full health.

To finely calibrate the scales, researchers may choose end-points representing two health states whose relative positions have been established in prior studies.

CONSIDER THE FOLLOWING LINE RANKING
HEALTH STATES ON A SCALE FROM 0 TO 1:

0	.25	.5	.75	1

Blindness   Occasional
                                                   blurred vision

Use a pencil to indicate where you would place the following health states on this line:

(1) frequent blurred vision (2) constant blurred vision.

By calibrating the scores for frequent and constant blurred vision against the already established scores for blindness and occasional blurred vision, researchers can develop consistent QALY scores for these additional conditions. For example, suppose surveys have established that blindness is worth 0.5 QALYs and occasional blurred vision is worth 0.9 QALYs. Now suppose that respondents place constant blurred vision at 0.5 on the aforementioned scale (that is, it is halfway between blindness and occasional blurred vision.) This means that constant blurred vision is worth 0.7 QALYs.

The relative scale approach is easy to describe and can even be conducted through the mail. However, the approach has two important weaknesses. First, it easily bogs down when the respondent must rank more than five health states. Second, respondents often get frustrated trying to place health states along the scale.[8] They have a qualitative "feel" for where to place a health state (e.g., blindness is pretty bad but not terrible), but they are often unable to decide among widely different placements (e.g., 0.4 to 0.8). This ambiguity makes mathematical manipulations of the scores somewhat tenuous.

To more rigorously quantify the QALY scores, researchers rely on one of two other approaches. Here is the *standard gamble approach*.[9] Once again, you can try this method yourself.

Consider the following alternatives:

1. You will be blind for the rest of your life
2. You will undergo a procedure to restore your vision. The procedure will be successful with probability p, where p is a number between 0 and 1. The procedure will fail with probability $1 - p$. If the procedure fails, you die instantly.

At what value of p are you indifferent between alternatives 1 and 2? _____

Many respondents are unfamiliar with the concept of indifference. To help them, researchers might ask whether the respondents would prefer the procedure to the certainty of blindness if the success rate of the procedure were 0.95. If a respondent prefers the procedure, then the researcher reduces the success rate to 0.9, and so forth. The point at which the respondent is unable to choose between the procedure and its risk of death and the certainty of blindness is the point of indifference.

Many respondents are also unfamiliar with probabilities. To help these respondents, researchers may use a probability wheel—a circle divided into two different-colored sections. For example, the researcher might show a wheel divided equally (50-50) into blue and yellow sections. The researcher would state that the outcome of the procedure depends on the spin of the wheel. If the respondent were indifferent between the certainty of blindness, or a procedure whose outcome depends on the spin of the wheel, then the point of indifference would be 0.5.

Here is how to convert your point of indifference to a QALY score. Suppose your point of indifference on the standard gamble question is 0.6. This means that you are indifferent between blindness for sure (giving you an as yet to be determined QALY score), a procedure that cures blindness 60 percent of the time (giving you a QALY score of 1), and kills you the rest of the time (for a score of 0). Some simple math shows that the procedure offers you an expected QALY score of 0.6.[10] By implication, you have given a QALY score for blindness of 0.6. More generally, the answer you gave to the standard gamble question is your QALY score for blindness.

The biggest advantage of the standard gamble approach is that the resulting QALY scores are derived from the same kinds of mathematical manipulations that are used to compute cost-effectiveness scores. The disadvantage is that some respondents may never fully grasp the concept of probabilities, and their responses may not reflect their true preferences.

The third approach is called the *time trade-off*. To understand the time-tradeoff-approach, we return to the prospect of living with blindness.

Consider the following alternatives:

1. You could live 50 more years with blindness, and then die.
2. You could live y more years in full health, and then die.

How big does y have to be for you to be indifferent between the two choices? _____

As with the standard gamble approach, the concept of indifference may confuse some respondents. The researcher might help out by asking whether the respondent would prefer to live 50 more years with blindness or 45 more years in full health. If the respondent prefers the latter, the researcher might offer the option of 40 years in full health, and so forth. The point at which the respondent cannot decide between the two options is the point of indifference.

Suppose your point of indifference is 20 years. In other words, you are indifferent between living 50 more years with blindness or 20 more years in full health. Since the latter option gives you 20 QALYs, you are implicitly giving blindness a QALY score of 0.4.[11] More generally, you can compute your time-trade-off QALY score for blindness by plugging your answer into the following formula: QALY = (your answer) ÷ 50.

There are well-documented differences in the QALY scores obtained using each approach. QALY scores seem to be highest using the standard gamble approach—most respondents balk at the risk of dying from the indicated surgery. These differences imply that league table rankings can be very sensitive to the choice of survey method. Concerned about possible biases that might result from relying on just one survey, many researchers prefer to use two or even all three survey approaches and average the QALY scores. In the above examples, the QALY scores for the relative scale, standard gamble, and time-trade-off approaches were 0.5, 0.6, and 0.4, respectively. Thus, the average QALY score for blindness would be 0.5.

How Do Your QALY Scores Measure Up?

Now that you know how QALYs are computed, let's see how your QALY scores for three health states measure up against those measured by researchers surveying the population at large. The health states to consider are

a. needs a walking stick
b. frequent vomiting
c. confined to bed with poor memory

Relative Scale. Use a pencil to indicate where you would place each of the three health states on this line:

0	.25	.5	.75	1

Dead   Full health

Now record the QALY scores for the three health states as indicated by their placement on the line.

QALY score using the relative scale approach:

a. need a walking stick _____
b. frequent vomiting _____
c. confined to bed with poor memory _____

Standard Gamble. Consider the following alternatives:

1. You will need a walking stick for the rest of your life.
2. You will undergo a procedure to restore you to full health. The procedure will be successful with probability p, where p is a number between 0 and 1. The procedure will fail with probability $1 - p$. If the procedure fails, you die instantly.

At what value of p are you indifferent between alternatives 1 and 2?

Repeat this question for "frequent vomiting" and "confined to bed with poor memory."

Now record your QALY scores for each health state. Remember, the probability that leaves you indifferent is your QALY score.

QALY score using the standard gamble approach:

a. needs a walking stick _____
b. frequent vomiting _____
c. confined to bed with poor memory _____

Time-Trade-Off Approach. Consider the following alternatives:

1. You could live 50 more years needing a walking stick, and then die.
2. You could live y more years in full health, and then die.

How big does y have to be for you to be indifferent between the two choices?

Repeat this question for "frequent vomiting" and "confined to bed with poor memory."

Now record your QALY scores for each health state. (If you answered y years, then your QALY score is given by the formula QALY = $y \div 50$.)

QALY score using the time-trade-off approach:

a. needs a walking stick _____
b. frequent vomiting _____
c. confined to bed with poor memory _____

Once you have completed all three approaches, enter your QALY scores in the appropriate cells in Table 6.5. Compute

TABLE 6.5   Your QALY Scores

(1) HEALTH STATE	(2) RELATIVE SCALE	(3) STANDARD GAMBLE	(4) TIME-TRADE-OFF	(5) AVERAGE (YOUR SCORES)	(6) REPORTED AVERAGE SCORES
Needs a walking stick					0.77
Frequent vomiting					0.57
Confined to bed with poor memory					0.30

the average score for each health state and record these values in column 5. These are your overall QALY scores for each health state. Column 6 lists the average scores based on surveys given to a cross-section of respondents and reported by Robert Kaplan, one of the pioneers of QALY research.[12]

THE QUALITY OF WELL-BEING (QWB) SCALE

The researchers who constructed the league table used by Oregon's Medicaid program based their rankings on a variant of the QALY approach called the Quality of Well-Being (QWB) scale. (Its European cousin is called the European Quality of Life [EuroQoL] scale.) Like QALYs, QWBs range from 0 (dead) to 1 (full health). Unlike QALYs, however, individuals do not directly score the health states. Instead, researchers use a two-step approach to measure QWBs.

In the first step, researchers ask medical experts to score health states on a number of dimensions. For example, one dimension of the EuroQoL is "mobility." The medical expert will assign the health state 1 point if there is no limitation in mobility associated with the health state, 2 points if there is moderate limitation, and 3 points if there is severe limitation. The EuroQoL has five health dimensions:

- mobility
- self-care
- usual activities
- pain/discomfort
- anxiety/depression

Experts assign each health state a score from 1 (best) to 3 (worst) for each dimension. Thus, "needs walking stick" might score 22211. Frequent vomiting might score 11233. All told, there are 243 different combinations of scores on the five health dimensions in the EuroQoL. Variants of this method, including the DALY approach used by the World Health Organization, can have over 1,000 combinations, depending on the number of dimensions and the range of point scores per dimension.

The second step is to survey the public to determine how to assign each combination a single score on a 0-to-1 scale. Researchers might begin by telling respondents that the combination 11111 scores 1 point, and death scores 0 points. They would then ask respondents to give point scores for 22211, 11233, and so forth. Respondents might say that 22211 is worth 0.75 points but that 11233 is worth only 0.40 points. Through statistical analysis, researchers can calculate the points for every combination. It is then a simple matter to assign a QWB score to a particular health state. If "needs a walking stick" scores 22211, and survey respondents give 0.75 points to 22211, then "needs a walking stick" scores 0.75 QWBs.

A big advantage of the QWB approach is that respondents do not have to know much about specific medical conditions. Instead, they only have to think about a few health dimensions. Medical experts make the connection between those dimensions and the actual health states. A disadvantage is that the handful of health dimensions may be insufficient to fully capture the essence of specific conditions. For example, blindness may score 22212 on the QWB health dimensions. This is almost identical to the score for "needs a walking stick," and the QWBs for both conditions would be similar. Yet most individuals would give a much lower QALY score to blindness.

Concerns about QALYs

Even big supporters acknowledge that the QALY approach is controversial. Two major concerns have to do with the potential to use QALYs for discrimination based on age and disability, and problems inherent in QALY survey methods.

DISCRIMINATION AND QALYS

The use of QALYs can lead to subtle and not-so-subtle discrimination in the allocation of health care dollars. Suppose a payer had to choose between providing coronary bypass surgery to a 50-year-old or a 90-year-old. On a cost-per-QALY basis, the choice is clear—the 50-year-old has a longer life expectancy and stands to gain far more QALYs. In the same manner, the QALY approach may discriminate against the disabled, many of whom also have shorter life expectancies.

Here is another, more subtle form of discrimination against the disabled. Consider the following plausible QALY scores:

Needs assistance walking	0.8
Blind	0.5
Needs assistance walking and blind	0.4

Now consider hip replacement surgery to help someone who needs assistance walking. With these scores, hip surgery for a blind person is worth 0.1 QALYs (the QALY score goes from 0.4 to 0.5). Hip surgery for a sighted person is worth 0.2 QALYs. Many people would be troubled by the notion that hip surgery is twice as valuable for sighted people than it is for blind people. Yet, by squeezing all scores between 0 and 1, we see that this will inevitably happen with QALY scores.

LIMITATIONS OF QALY SURVEYS

The stakes involved in QALY research are huge—literally billions of dollars may ride on a single QALY score. The fact that QALY scores depend on survey research ought to give one pause. Researchers may use a variety of techniques to influence survey responses, including judicious selection of respondents, wording of questions, and handling of unusual responses. With so much riding on the outcome of QALY surveys, it should be no surprise that there are countless books and academic articles offering advice about how to construct valid QALY scores. At the same time, academic journals carefully scrutinize survey methods prior to publication of QALY papers. As a result, survey methods are continually improving.

Concerns about the integrity of QALY surveys should probably be discounted.

Unfortunately, valid survey methods do not guarantee usable survey responses. If the purpose of QALY surveys is to determine the value of specific health states, then it is somewhat disturbing to note that most survey respondents have no experience with those health states. What, then, should we make of their responses? A number of studies show that healthy individuals give lower QALY scores for various health states than do individuals who have those conditions. For example, sighted people may give blindness a QALY score of 0.5, but blind people may give it a score of 0.7. Apparently, healthy individuals overestimate the emotional impact and physical limitations of being ill.[13]

One way to bring the QALY scores more in line is to provide healthy respondents with more information about each health state. Unfortunately, research shows that information overload can bias responses—the more detail, the lower the score! Another solution is to survey only physicians or patients who have experience with the health state. However, it can then be difficult to obtain a large enough sample of respondents.

A related problem is that QALY scores are often inconsistent across nations and across cultures. One study comparing the United Kingdom and Spain found significant differences in scores for about one-third of the health states, with some reversals of rankings. This means that policymakers in one country should be careful about using QALY scores from surveys conducted in another country.

SUMMING UP CEA/CBA METHODS

Chapters 5 and 6 have described the basic steps in analyzing the cost-effectiveness of health care interventions.

1. *Identify how an intervention affects the course of treatment and outcomes.* Ideally, researchers will use

randomized double-blind trials to minimize potential biases.

2. *Measure the benefits*. Most interventions do more than just save lives. Other health benefits must be scored using QALYs or a similar measure.

3. *Quantify the benefits using QALY scores*. Researchers may have to develop new QALY scores for specific disease states and populations.

4. *Measure the costs*. Providers' cost-accounting systems are often inadequate, and there is considerable disagreement about how to treat future costs. Unfortunately, researchers have not devoted the same attention to cost measurement as they have to benefit measurement.

5. *Apply a discount rate*. Future costs and benefits should be discounted. There is no consensus about how to choose the discount rate. Small differences can lead to very different conclusions about the cost-effectiveness of some interventions.

6. *Compute the benefit/cost ratio and compare it with established norms*. Researchers often report their findings in league tables.

Despite the many limitations that I have discussed, the methods for computing cost-effectiveness and for constructing league tables are well accepted and in widespread use. The academic journal *Medical Decision Making* is devoted to advancing CEA methods, and many other journals publish CEA studies. The QALY approach is firmly established as the methodology of choice for cost-effectiveness research.

WHAT ABOUT THE PSA TEST?

Following the steps laid out above, a research team at the University of Toronto computed the cost per QALY of the PSA test for prostate cancer.[14] The team consulted previously published research to determine how PSA test results affected the course of treatment and outcomes. Using the time-trade-off approach, they surveyed urologists, radiation oncologists, and internists to determine the QALY scores for incontinence and impotence. Putting the pieces together, they found that the PSA test increased life expectancy, but it also increased the chances of incontinence and impotence. At a discount rate of 5 percent, the PSA test did not appear to increase QALYs at all. In the most optimistic scenario, the QALY increase is modest, and the cost per QALY exceeds $250,000.

These kinds of analyses are becoming more common in medicine, and there is even a chance that decisions about your medical care might be based on QALY methods. Beginning a decade ago, regulators in Oregon attempted to impose QALY methods on the entire Medicaid population. Chapter 7 describes this sweeping application of rational rationing methods.

ENDNOTES

1. M. Krahn et al., 1994, "Screening for Prostate Cancer: A Decision Analytic View," *Journal of the American Medical Association* 272(10): 773–80.

2. G. Torrance, W. Thomas, and D. Sackett, 1972, "A Utility Maximization Model for Evaluation of Health Care Programmes," *Health Services Research* 7(2): 118–33.

3. R. Kaplan, 1996, "Utility Assessment for Estimating Quality-Adjusted Life Years," in F. Sloan, ed., *Valuing Health Care,* Cambridge: Cambridge University Press.

4. This is because $(0.5 \times 1) + (0.5 \times 0.5) = 0.75$.

5. The data are fictitious, but hopefully they illustrate the general idea behind the use of QALYs.

6. Note that this example ignores discounting, which can complicate the calculations considerably.

7. C. Phillips and G. Thompson, 1998, "What Is a QALY?" Newmarket, UK: Hayward Medical Communications. R. Chapman et al., 2000, "A Comprehensive League Table of Cost–Utility Ratios and a Sub-table of 'Panel-Worthy' Studies," *Medical Decision Making* 20: 451–67. Reprinted by permission of publisher. Note that the reported figures have been rounded.

8. G. Torrance, D. Feeney, and W. Furlong, 2001, "Visual Analog Scales," *Medical Decision Making* 21: 329–34.

9. For a good detailed description of how to implement the standard gamble approach, see M. Drummond, G. Stoddard, and G. Torrance, 1987, *Methods for the Economic Evaluation of Health Care Programmes,* Oxford: Oxford University Press.

10. Using the law of expectations, we can compute that the expected QALY score is $(0.6 \times 1) + (0.4 \times 0) = 0.6$.

11. 0.4 QALYs per year × 50 years gives you 20 QALYs. Again, this ignored discounting.

12. Kaplan, ibid.

13. For example, see P. Ubel et al., 2001, "Do Nonpatients Underestimate the Quality of Life Associated with Chronic Health Conditions Because of a Focusing Illusion?" *Medical Decision Making* 21(3): 190–99.

14. Krahn et al., ibid.

7 THE OREGON PLAN

During the 1980s, health services researchers advanced the frontiers of cost-effectiveness research. Cost-effectiveness studies appeared in all the major medical journals. Occasionally, a meta-analysis in some prestigious journal even caused wholesale changes in medical practice. Yet patients remained largely unaware of the increasing role of CEA. In the state of Oregon in 1989, however, the behind-the-scenes science of CEA was exposed to the very open politics of rationing. The result serves as a warning to anyone attempting to institutionalize rational rationing: Science and politics do not always mix.

RATIONING IN OREGON

Oregon explicitly rations services for Medicaid patients. Each year, the state publishes a "priority list" of about 740 condition-treatment pairs, such as drug therapy for pneumonia. The pairs are ranked from most to least cost-effective. Once the rankings are in, the state draws a line across the list. The line is currently drawn at treatment 566 (treatment of dysfunction of the tear ducts). The state refuses to pay for treatments below that line. If Medicaid patients want treatments that fall below the line, they will need to come up with the money themselves, or convince their providers to provide them free of charge. Many patients, if not most, end up doing without.

Rationing of Medicaid patients might seem like the handiwork of Republicans seeking to balance the budget on the backs of low-income Medicaid recipients. Yet Oregon's largely middle-class population leans to the left of the political spectrum and has supported many legislative initiatives that more conservative states usually reject. When rationing was proposed, Democrats controlled all branches of the state government. Moreover, John Kitzhaber, then president of the state senate and the politician most responsible for the Oregon plan, was a liberal Democrat.

It seems surprising that such a progressive state would embrace a scheme that would be condemned by liberal groups around the nation. Tennessee Senator Al Gore decried the Oregon plan as "a declaration of unconditional surrender" at a time when there was a great national debate about the future of the health care system.[1] But there have been bipartisan concerns about Medicaid costs ever since the inception of the program in 1965. Medicaid, which was part of President Lyndon Johnson's Great Society program, pays for health care services for the "categorically needy." This means that recipients must not only be poor, but they must also belong to one of several categories to be eligible: disabled, blind, elderly, or families with dependent children. Unlike the Medicare program, which most Americans view almost as a birthright, Medicaid is usually thought of as a welfare program.

Like other welfare programs, Medicaid is partially funded by the federal government. But it is up to each state to determine how to implement Medicaid (subject to some federal rules and restrictions) and come up with the rest of the funding. Almost from the outset, states suffered under the burden of higher-than-expected Medicaid costs. Some staunchly liberal states, including New York, Massachusetts, and Wisconsin, had large Medicaid populations and correspondingly high costs. These states tried raising taxes to cover the costs, but even Democratic taxpayers have their limits. So, during the

1970s, legislators tried a variety of regulations to ease the tax burden.

None of the regulations worked. Limits on hospital payments managed to reduce expenditure increases by about 1 percentage point at best. Restrictions on hospital expansion failed when hospitals found ways to skirt the rules. Through the 1970s and 1980s, Medicaid cost growth continued to outstrip tax revenues. By the late 1980s, Medicaid accounted for 10 percent of the typical state's budget, making it the second-largest state expenditure (behind education). In the words of one analyst, Medicaid had become "the monster that ate the states."[2] In an era dominated by President Reagan's conservative ideology, even progressive states felt the pressure to hold the line on taxes. With Medicaid costs still growing and tax revenues holding steady, something had to give.

The recession of the early 1980s struck Oregon particularly hard; further tax increases to support Medicaid were out of the question. Oregon had to consider other ways to reduce Medicaid costs. The state had three options. It could shift enrollees into managed care, reduce enrollments, or eliminate services. Like many states, Oregon experimented with all three. During the 1980s, the state moved about half of its Medicaid enrollees into HMOs. At the same time, it tightened eligibility requirements. By the late 1980s, Oregon's Medicaid plan covered fewer than 60 percent of residents living below the poverty level. Finally, and most controversially, the state limited coverage of certain costly services, including transplant services.

Many state Medicaid programs, Oregon among them, began covering transplants in the 1980s. Like other states, Oregon soon ran into budget problems. In 1987, Oregon's Department of Human Resources requested $2.2 million to fund 34 "high-risk" Medicaid transplants (for bone marrow, pancreas, heart, and liver). The state's Ways and Means Committee determined that the only way to fund this request was to take the money from a special $20 million budget earmarked for social programs. But these programs, which dealt with the mentally ill, juvenile delinquents, and other social problems, had substantial political support. The committee decided to keep the programs intact. Oregon thus joined at least 15 other state Medicaid plans by limiting access to transplants.

The decision to ration the access of low-income Medicaid patients to transplants drew support from several grassroots organizations, including the highly regarded Oregon Health Decisions.[3] Oregon Health Decisions had been lobbying the legislature for a decade to find ways to expand access to the uninsured, and the group hoped that the resources freed up by rationing would help. No one in the state legislature questioned the decision to ration transplants. But, a few months after the final budget was approved in July 1987, events unfolded that would make some legislators regret their vote.

THE STORY OF COBY HOWARD

In the autumn of 1987, 7-year-old Coby Howard's leukemia came out of remission. A bone marrow transplant would give the Oregon boy a 20 percent chance of surviving, but Coby's mom was unemployed and on welfare, and Medicaid would not pay for the $100,000 procedure. The Howards' friends and neighbors tried to raise the money through bowl-a-thons and garage sales. The local press ran regular "Coby Howard updates." Amid all the attention, Coby Howard became an unwilling celebrity. The patrons at a restaurant even pressed him to get up on stage and sing "Rudolph the Red-Nosed Reindeer"! By the scheduled date of the operation, November 25, the Howards had raised enough money to go ahead with the surgery, but leukemia cells had spread through Coby's bone marrow. The operation was postponed, the cancer never went back into remission, and Coby Howard died in his mother's arms on December 2.

Several other Medicaid patients were also affected by Oregon's new policy. Donna Arneson needed a liver transplant. Her 14-year-old son Evan appeared before the state legislature, pleading with them to "save my mom." This spurred the "Save a Mom" campaign, complete with posters and videos, which raised enough money to pay for the operation. Two-year-old David Holladay needed a bone marrow transplant. His mom packed the entire family into a pickup truck and moved to Washington state, which pays for organ transplants and has no minimum residency requirement for Medicaid. Another woman needing a liver transplant went to San Francisco, where a hospital performed it free of charge.

The news of what was happening in Oregon spread throughout the nation. *The New York Times, Washington Post*, and *Los Angeles Times* put Coby Howard on the front page. The *Washington Post* headline was perhaps the most telling: "Rising Cost of Medical Treatment Forces Oregon to 'Play God.'"[4] Just a few weeks after the state had quietly blocked funding for transplants, it faced an unexpected political firestorm. Forced to defend its policy, a spokesperson for the state's Medicaid program pointed out that the money it had spent on 34 transplants in 1987 would instead be used to pay for four other programs, including prenatal care for 1,500 pregnant women.[5] The issue, she said, was one of doing the greatest good with the limited resources at hand. In other words, the decision to block funding of transplants was cost-effective.

This defense did not satisfy everyone. In January 1988, members of the state legislature attempted to restore $220,000 in funding for five Medicaid patients awaiting transplants. The proposal was forwarded to a committee chaired by state Senate President John Kitzhaber. Kitzhaber, who was an emergency room physician before turning to politics, and a defender of the decision to block funding for transplants, would now take center stage in the rationing debate.

TOWARD A RATIONAL RATIONING PLAN

In the short time after Coby Howard's death, opponents of the transplant policy attempted to frame the debate in terms of wealth versus health. Oregon, they said, was too stingy to save lives. Kitzhaber reframed the debate in terms of equity.

Arguing against the restoration of funding, he pointed out that many Oregonians lacked insurance altogether, and that opponents were asking taxpayers to purchase health care services for Medicaid patients that they could not afford to buy for their own families.[6]

Kitzhaber took the debate one step further. Using the language of CEA, he argued in favor of using limited Medicaid funds to save as many lives as possible, because "we can't save them all."[7] The motion to restore funding failed on a tie vote, with Kitzhaber voting against it. That evening, John Kitzhaber appeared on the popular television news show *Nightline*. Echoing the *Washington Post*, host Ted Koppel wondered whether Oregon's legislators were "playing God." The next day, Kitzhaber spoke to the state legislature, acknowledging that Oregon was "going to have to ration health care."[8]

THE CREATION OF THE OREGON HEALTH PLAN

The first order of business for Kitzhaber and the Oregon legislature was to win the public relations battle. Kitzhaber advanced two arguments in favor of developing a rationing plan. The first was that Oregon, like all other states, was already rationing care by limiting enrollments and payments to providers.[9] The decision not to fund transplants was simply more transparent and better publicized than other forms of rationing. The second argument was that Oregon and other states had not done an effective job of rationing and that as a result, too many people were dying. He refined earlier cost-effectiveness arguments, stating that spending the money on transplants might save as many as 12 lives in one year, but redirecting the money to prenatal care could instead save 25 infants.

The media caught on to the language of cost-effectiveness. Newspapers reported the potential for the plan to save lives. One East Coast paper began an article on the Oregon plan by offering the following choice: Should state lawmakers spend $100,000 on a bone marrow transplant for an elderly man or immunize 10,000 children against measles?[10] Having framed the debate his way, Kitzhaber had temporarily won the public relations battle. Now he had to come up with a plan.

By all accounts, Kitzhaber was solely responsible for drafting the legislation that would become the Oregon Health Plan. After the vote to block additional transplant funding, Kitzhaber convinced his colleagues to create a new Senate Committee on Health Insurance and Bioethics that he would chair. The committee held extensive hearings through the first half of 1989, in which scientists, providers, and citizens' groups aired their views. The major area of contention was the trade-off between access and benefits. Despite the public debate and vocal opposition to any form of explicit rationing, this was Kitzhaber's show, and in the end, he got what he wanted.

Kitzhaber's first goal was to expand access, and he insisted that Oregon's Medicaid plan cover all residents with incomes below the poverty level. His second goal was to free up the funds to expand access by denying payments for services that were not cost-effective. Many critics were concerned that the proposal might result in inadequate benefits for everyone. Kitzhaber made one fateful concession—he restricted the legislation to families with dependent children. Other Medicaid beneficiaries—he elderly, the blind, and the disabled—were exempted.

THE OREGON PLAN AND HMOS

Although it received very little attention from the media, an interesting sidebar to the rationing debate involved HMOs. By the late 1980s, half of all Oregon Medicaid recipients were in HMOs. (Almost all are in HMOs today.) Medicaid HMOs were generally more restrictive than private sector HMOs and had already saved the state a considerable amount of money. But the state's rationing scheme was expected to save even more. For Medicaid recipients who were enrolled in HMOs, the state did not deny payments per se. Instead, it cut payments to HMOs by an amount equal to the projected savings from rationing. Most HMOs cited this policy to justify refusing to pay for the services proscribed by the state. By inference, the state's rationing scheme would be more restrictive than any rationing done by the Medicaid HMOs.

CREATING THE LIST

The most controversial piece of Kitzhaber's plan was the creation of the prioritized list of health services. Services with high benefits and low costs would head the list. Low-benefit, high-cost services would be placed at the bottom. The state would draw a line on the list and refuse to pay for services below the line. The money that would have been spent on those services would instead be used to expand enrollments. The bill was enacted in June 1989 with very little opposition. The "easy" part was over. Now Oregon had to create the list.

The legislature established a Health Services Commission to do the work. The 11-member commission included 5 physicians and 2 other health care professionals. Over the next few months, the commission, along with Oregon Health Decisions, conducted 11 public hearings and almost 50 town meetings to learn how Oregonians felt about health care. In all, over 1,000 Oregonians—mostly well-educated health care workers—took part. The commission learned that the people who attended the hearings and meetings valued prevention, cost-effectiveness, quality of life, and longevity. These were hardly revelations. Nor was this enough information to enable the commission to create the list. That would require input from experts versed in CEA.

The commission turned for help to Robert Kaplan, a physician at the University of California in San Diego. Kaplan had recently developed the Quality of Well-Being (QWB) scale. Recall from Chapter 6 that in developing the QWB scale, experts rated medical conditions on several health dimensions such as mobility and pain. Following this approach, the commission formed a medical committee that identified more than 1,600 condition-treatment pairs, such as medical therapy for osteoporosis and nutritional counseling for obesity. The committee then scored the health benefits of each of the conditions on the QWB health dimensions.

The next step was to ask individuals in the community to convert the multidimensional score for each condition into a single score between 0 and 1. Kaplan and his colleague John Anderson had already created such scores based on interviews with residents of California. The commission decided not to use these scores, and instead asked Oregon State University to conduct a telephone survey of 1,000 Oregon residents. On the basis of how Oregonians valued different health dimensions, the commission computed the QWB improvement for each of the 1,600 condition-treatment pairs. At the same time, the commission computed the costs of each of the treatments and the resulting cost-effectiveness values.

For example, the commission found that the typical treatment of botulism resulted in a QWB improvement of 0.3 per year, which would last for an average of 40 years. Thus, botulism treatment generated an overall (undiscounted) gain of 12 QWBs. The average cost of botulism treatment was about $96. Thus, the cost per QWB for botulism treatment was about $8. On May 2, 1990, the commission published its prioritized list of 1,600 condition-treatment pairs. Based on its relatively low cost per QWB, botulism treatment was near the top of the list.

Many of the other rankings were counterintuitive. Treatment for thumb sucking ranked above hospitalization of a child for starvation. Treatment of sleep disorders, viral herpes, varicose veins, and impacted teeth ranked near the bottom. So did treatment of late-stage AIDS. The already skeptical news media heaped scorn upon the rankings. Senator Gore published an op-ed piece in the *Los Angeles Times* whose lead sentence read, "Imagine a health-care system in which only quadriplegics can get dentures and those in need of teeth to eat are issued a blender and the name of a nutritionist."[11] Craig Irwin, the head of the Oregon Transplant Project, said it was "absurd" to rank liver transplants lower than reconstructive breast surgery.[12]

How could the rankings seem so wrong? Part of the problem was that the QWB approach asks about a limited number of health dimensions rather than the conditions themselves. The result is that some rather unwelcome conditions, such as impacted teeth, score well on each of the QWB conditions. Treatment for these conditions produce only modest QWB increases and low benefit/cost ratios. Another problem was that some treatments, such as hospitalization of a starving child, had less costly alternatives that were almost equally effective. The new reports emphasized the low rankings without mentioning the alternatives. Yet another problem was that treatment of some low-QWB conditions, such as late-stage AIDS, was almost completely ineffective. Although the public perceived that such treatment was worthwhile, the fact remained that it was very costly and had an extremely low benefit/cost ratio. But part of the blame fell squarely on the Health Services Commission, which admitted that it had used some wildly inaccurate cost figures. Many of the rankings—no one knew just how many—were simply wrong.

The rankings were published with considerable fanfare on May 2, 1990. A front-page story in *The New York Times* quoted Richard Lamm, a health care activist and former governor of Colorado, expressing his admiration for the Oregon legislature having the "guts" to craft a health care policy that would bring the most good to the most people. Lamm further opined that other states would inevitably have to follow Oregon's lead.[13] An editorial in *The New York Times* called the plan a "brave medical experiment."[14]

On May 3, the commission disowned the rankings, claiming it had only been "testing" the methodology. Commission Chair Harvey Klevit backpedaled as fast as anyone; after looking at the first two pages, he "threw it in the trash can."[15] By August 1990, the commission had formed a subcommittee to develop a new list. Oregon's first attempt to implement rational rationing was on hold. Scientific methods (albeit compromised by some questionable cost data) bumped up against intuition, and science lost.

THE NEW LIST

The subcommittee decided to make the rankings more intuitive. It divided conditions into several categories based on whether they were treatable and their consequences if left untreated. The highest priority was given to treatments that would cure conditions that were acute and potentially fatal, such as appendicitis and whooping cough. Lower priority was given to treatments that would improve the quality of life, such as hip replacement surgery and corneal transplants. Treatments that did not improve the quality of life or extend life, such as aggressive treatment of end-stage cancer or treatments known to be ineffective, received the lowest priority. In addition, the commission discounted quantitative information about QWBs and costs, relying more on its own "values and judgments" to create the rankings.[16]

Several months of political give-and-take followed. Some commission members wanted to give high priority to virtually all preventive services, in keeping with the preferences of Oregonians surveyed the year before. They succeeded in placing several preventive services above the line. But physicians on the commission doubted the effectiveness of nutritional supplements and dental checkups and wanted to raise the rankings of several costly surgeries. The physicians lost that battle. Winners and losers aside, it was clear that in "massaging" the priority list, the commission was sometimes willing to let science take a back seat to politics.

In February 1991, the Health Services Commission published its new list. By grouping treatments, the commission managed to reduce the list to 709 condition-treatment pairs. Despite the political give-and-take, the rankings on the consolidated list bore a close resemblance to the rankings on the original list. Proponents of the original list, including Robert Kaplan, expressed their support for the changes. At the same time, the new list seemed far more intuitive. The treatments at the top of the list looked like they belonged there; the treatments at the bottom deserved to be at the bottom.[17]

At the top of the list were medical treatments for bacterial pneumonia and tuberculosis. Appendectomies, repair of ruptured intestines, and surgery for ectopic pregnancy (in which the fetus develops outside the womb) also made the top 10. Without any doubt, these treatments had very high benefit/cost ratios. The middle of the list included routine and well-accepted treatments such as medical therapy for sinusitis and repair of open wounds. Life support for anencephaly ranked last. Other condition-treatment pairs at the bottom of the list included life support for extremely low birthweight babies and medical therapy for end-stage AIDS. These costly treatments provided no lasting benefit. The fact that they were provided at all was reflective of the inherent inefficiencies in the Medicaid program.

The commission drew the line at condition-treatment pair 566—breast reconstruction for absence of breast after mastectomy.[18] (Shortly thereafter, the state expanded the list to 745 condition-treatment pairs and redrew the line accordingly.) Treatments below this line—treatments that had such low benefit/cost ratios that the state felt they were not worth providing—accounted for 10 percent of all Medicaid expenditures. By eliminating payments for these treatments, the state could free up funds to expand coverage. Oregon was almost ready to put the list into practice.

MORE PROTESTS

Although the state had quieted critics who found the initial list unintuitive, it had done nothing to quell critics who were opposed to any form of explicit rationing. If anything, the controversy over the rankings invigorated opponents. Noted economist Henry Aaron observed that when it comes to rationing, "You'd better get it right" because it is sure to raise a "lot of heat."[19] A lot of heat was applied by patients and providers directly affected by the plan. Citing the potential reduction in funding for AIDS treatment, one AIDS activist called it "the Oregon death plan."[20] Physicians whose services fell just below the line also complained. (For example, orthopedic surgeons complained because some back surgeries were excluded.) But the Oregon Medical Association supported the plan and the American Medical Association remained neutral. It turned out that bone marrow and other transplants were above the line, helping to quiet the "Coby Howard" contingent. One cannot help but wonder if the placement of these treatments above the line was based on cost-effectiveness analysis or politics.

Some of the most heated criticism of the plan came not from particular patients or providers, but rather from liberals who had been fighting for a decade or more to increase Medicaid funding. Political activists argued that Oregon spent a far lower percentage of its budget on Medicaid than did many other states. Senator Gore observed that the state could expand enrollments by 250,000 simply by increasing its percentage commitment to equal that of other states. Why ration at all, the critics seemed to be asking.

Another wave of protests, led by the Children's Defense Fund and Families USA as well as Senator Gore, focused on the fact that the Oregon plan was restricted to Medicaid families with dependent children. Elderly Medicaid enrollees were exempted, as were all privately insured patients. An aide to Senator Gore complained that Oregon was "singling out poor women and children."[21] The state argued that it faced difficult choices about how to spend Medicaid dollars, and the rationing plan assured the biggest benefit. Sociologist Lawrence Brown scoffed at this claim, arguing that if the state really wanted to make hard choices, it could impose the rationing scheme on state employees, including legislators.[22] The Gore aide echoed this sentiment, wondering if the state planned to let Medicaid children die so that it could afford to provide medical care to the children of state employees.[23]

These critics had a bigger agenda, to assure equal access for all patients through a nationalized health care system. But they were deluding themselves if they believed that the alternative to the Oregon plan was a national plan with universal coverage. A national health care system was not on the horizon back in 1991 (despite widespread debate, President Clinton's plan never came up for a vote in Congress), and it remains a pipe dream to this day. In terms of access, the alternative to the Oregon plan was the status quo or worse, as the subsequent experiences of virtually every other Medicaid plan have shown. Objections on high-minded ideological grounds did nothing to assure that Oregon's poor would get the medical services they needed most. If anything, it was unfair to ask Oregon's poor to endure the inefficiencies and inequities of the old Medicaid plan while academics and politicians continued their decades-old debate about national health insurance.

Even if the United States adopted a national health insurance plan, this would hardly do away with rationing. The experiences of patients in Canada, England, Australia, Germany, and elsewhere suggest that national health care simply extends rationing to the entire population. And with growing private insurance markets in many of these nations, nationalized systems are no longer even equitable.

Critics of the plan also objected on technical grounds. Some of their concerns had merit. Sometimes, disparate illnesses were aggregated into a single condition-treatment pair. For example, different stages of breast cancer were treated as a homogeneous condition. As a result, the rankings ignored potentially large differences in the medical needs of patients. The cost data were still poor. One of the most stinging criticisms was that Medicaid recipients had virtually no input into the creation of the list. Kaplan produced evidence that QWB scores seem to be independent of socioeconomic status, suggesting that the list could apply equally well to all Oregonians. Despite this evidence, protestors maintained that the voice of the poor had not been heard.

None of these complaints really mattered. Kitzhaber understood that any rationing plan would have technical limitations, so that fixing some of the existing problems would not quiet the critics. Kitzhaber also understood that if the plan could stand up to withering criticism on issues of fairness, it could surely stand up to complaints about arguments that most citizens would view as technicalities. The majority of Oregonians continued to support the plan. (A poll found that the majority of Americans outside of Oregon were opposed, however.) His popularity on the rise, Kitzhaber held his ground, and the state moved closer to implementing his plan.

There was one more hurdle to clear. The federal Health Care Finance Administration (HFCA) has final say over any major changes to state Medicaid plans and would have to approve the rationing scheme before Oregon could put it into practice. In early 1992, HCFA stopped the plan dead in its tracks, stating that it violated the Americans with Disabilities Act of 1990. (Some have conjectured that President George H. W. Bush torpedoed the plan because he did not want to campaign against Bill Clinton as the "rationing president."[24]) HCFA claimed that the QWB scale discriminated against the disabled, because their lives were "worth" less than fully healthy lives and their medical care would generate smaller QWB gains. Robert Kaplan responded that this analysis "was not only misinformed, it was incorrect."[25] He noted, correctly, that life-extending treatments generate substantial QWB gains, even for patients with disabilities, and would invariably end up "above the line." Moreover, healthy people need fewer services and would not take resources away from the disabled.

Oregon decided not to debate the issue. The state abandoned efforts to quantify benefits on a single scale such as QWB. From then on, rankings would be qualitative—a kind of "informed judgment" of where treatments ought to be ranked. Treatments were valued solely on the basis of whether they extended life and alleviated symptoms. Despite this major change, 85 percent of the rankings in the newest scale were close to the original rankings. In March 1993, HCFA approved the revised plan, and in February 1994, the plan became a reality. In November 1994, Kitzhaber won a narrow victory to become the governor of Oregon.

THE PERFORMANCE OF THE RATIONING PLAN

The Oregon plan appears to have been an instant success. Every Oregonian with income below the poverty line became immediately eligible for Medicaid. An additional 100,000 residents enrolled in the program, representing a 39 percent increase in the Medicaid population. As a result, the state's uninsured fell to 11 percent of the total population, even as the national rate was increasing to 15 percent.[26] In addition to expanding enrollments, the state also expanded coverage. In 1995, the state added chemical dependency services for all enrollees and mental health services for 25 percent of enrollees. Mental health coverage went statewide in 1997. Medicaid recipients were also covered for dental care.

Unfortunately, time has taken its toll on the Oregon plan. The state remains committed to reducing the number of uninsured. But, while the rationing plan initially freed up resources to expand Medicaid enrollments, it did nothing to stem growth in health care cost. To make matters worse, physicians have become increasingly adept at finding ways around the seemingly strict rules of the plan. In many cases, physicians are able to alter their diagnoses or their treatment recommendations to move a case above the line and make it eligible for reimbursement. Many physicians who would not resort to such "gaming" of the system still feel obligated to treat patients who fall below the line. Such charity reduces their incomes, which intensifies pressure on the state to raise reimbursement rates. The end result of all of these forces has been intense pressure on the Medicaid budget.

The state has responded by raising the line, once from 606 to 578, and then again to 574. Each time, it had to obtain approval from HCFA, which was no easy task. At one point, Oregon officials "spent hours arguing about diaper rash" before getting permission to move it below the line.[27] By 2001, Governor Kitzhaber was proposing to raise the line to 563. Some treatable cancers, and treatments for poison ivy and genital warts, would no longer be funded. To further balance the books, the state has asked some Medicaid recipients to pay a small premium of up to $360 annually. In response to these cutbacks, some in the news media have suggested that the Oregon plan was faltering.[28]

Such criticism is undeserved. Oregon's failure to contain health care costs is not unique and is certainly not the fault of its rationing scheme. All states have felt the pain of rising Medicaid costs and have coped in different ways, such as reducing payments to providers, raising patient copayments, tightening eligibility requirements, and shifting enrollees into managed care. The end result is always more rationing. Whatever the scientific merits of its prioritized list, Oregon remains the only state willing to explicitly ration on the basis of cost-effectiveness (or some intuitive version of cost-effectiveness). In this regard, Oregon has remained true to its mission, and its Medicaid program remains popular among taxpayers and beneficiaries alike.

Colorado is the only other state to consider a similar approach. In 1998, a state commission studied five different Medicaid programs and concluded that Oregon's program offered the best way to expand enrollments and contain costs. Echoing John Kitzhaber's comments from a decade earlier, the chairman of the state's Commission on Life and the Law acknowledged that "health care rationing [was] already going on" in Colorado and favored replacing implicit rationing with explicit rationing.[29] The commission report made the front pages of Colorado newspapers, but the idea went nowhere in the state legislature.

OREGON TEN YEARS LATER

When John Kitzhaber began crafting the Oregon plan, the health services research community was buzzing with excitement. Years of work developing and refining CEA methodologies would finally be put into practice. Moreover, the Oregon plan was front-page news. The entire nation, forced to confront the truth about the pervasiveness of implicit rationing, would be watching. Proponents of explicit rationing had crunched the numbers and knew that their approach would save lives and money. With Oregon leading the way, surely the rest of the nation would embrace their scientific approach to reining in health care costs. Or so went the thinking at the time.

Today, researchers look on the Oregon plan with mixed feelings. Though still guided by the principle of cost-effectiveness, the state's Health Services Commission has abandoned many of the main precepts of CEA. After treatments have been ranked according to both their costs and their ability to prevent death, further rankings are purely subjective, although the subjective criteria at least bear an intuitive link to scientific cost-effectiveness criteria. (For example, the subjective criteria include "medical ineffectiveness," "self-limiting conditions," and "prevent future costs.") But gone are QWBs and explicit benefit/cost calculations. Condition-treatment pairs appear above or below the line because such rankings make intuitive sense, not because they are scientifically valid. Moreover, much of the savings appears to come from the "low-hanging fruit"—those services for which there is no documented evidence of effectiveness. Oregon had avoided many of the hard choices that a strictly scientific approach to CEA would make.

Science lost out to intuition for several reasons. The methods themselves were partly to blame. Because good cost data were lacking and because many conditions were lumped together into broad categories, it was inevitable that the resulting priority list would have some counterintuitive rankings and engender controversy. But even if the methods were carried out to perfection, the rankings were sure to surprise some people and rankle others. After all, the public routinely misperceives benefits and risks and has little information about costs. CEA proponents should expect substantial objections and even ridicule for some of their work. But bowing to public pressure as they did—the initial priority list survived just one day under the political microscope—allows poorly formed opinions to replace scientific inquiry as the basis for public policy.

Perhaps there was little the scientists could do to defend their proposal. Although Kitzhaber had a deep understanding of CEA methods, the rest of the Oregon legislature was rather ill informed about the scientific merits of the priority list. Moreover, the Health Services Commission itself was uneasy with the initial list and was undoubtedly more than happy to impose its own version of CEA on the revised list. This decision ensured that the legislature, rather than scientists, remained in control of the flow of Medicaid funds.

Despite the intrusion of politics, the revised priority list was still based in cost-effectiveness principles, and it retained the support of Robert Kaplan and other leading CEA scholars. But the list suffered another blow when put up to its second political challenge, passing muster with the federal HCFA. President Bush could not afford to start a debate about health care rationing when candidate Bill Clinton had made health care reform a centerpiece of his campaign. So, any semblance of scientific methods in Oregon's plan fell victim to national politics. Today, the list remains as much a political statement as a scientific one.

Ironically, Clinton's plan would have pushed all Americans into managed care plans that use nonprice rationing. At the same time, the plan would have established a federal commission to evaluate the cost-effectiveness of new technologies. Republicans made effective use of Americans' concerns about this kind of rationing to kill the Clinton plan and take control of Congress in 1994.

WHERE DO WE DRAW THE LINE?

Lost in the controversy about the use of scientific methods was any discussion about where to draw the line. Critics wanted no line at all. The state of Oregon drew the line by setting a budget and seeing how much health care it could afford to buy. The line is currently drawn at service 574. Services just below the line, such as medical treatment of pelvic pain (line 582), do provide some benefit. But the state does not pay for them. This is not because the state believes the costs exceed the benefits. It is doubtful that anyone in the legislature has ever attempted to perform such a benefit/cost analysis. The state draws the line at service 574 for one simple reason: There is no money in the current budget to pay for service 575.

True rational rationing programs take a different approach to drawing the line. Rather than fix the budget and see how far it goes, other nations have established cost-effectiveness thresholds and seem willing to pay for drugs and other interventions that meet them. England's NICE has consistently recommended in favor of interventions with costs per QALY below £20,000 (about $30,000) and against interventions with costs per QALY above £50,000 (about $75,000). In Australia, the comparable thresholds are $13,000 and $65,000 in U.S. dollars. Canada advocates similar thresholds, though it is less than explicit in their application. If these nations stick to their thresholds, then their health care budgets may go up or down depending on the cost-effectiveness of new technologies. This raises a vital question: Are these reasonable thresholds?

To answer this question is to determine how much life is worth. Some payers seem to have already answered this question. The governments in England, Canada, and Australia will definitely spend up to $20,000 or $30,000 of their taxpayers' money so that one citizen can gain 1 QALY. However, they are unwilling to spend more than $65,000 to $75,000 for 1 additional QALY. By implication, they must believe that a life-year is worth somewhere between $20,000 and $75,000.

Is a year of an Australian's life worth no more than $65,000? Should Britons and Canadians be happy that their governments will spend no more than this amount to save lives? Many people would claim that there is no way to answer these questions, no way to explicitly put a dollar value on life. They argue that establishing thresholds on spending must therefore be a political decision. Unfortunately, this argument could be used to defend drawing the line in Oregon at service 700 or service 500, or for that matter at service 50. It could justify NICE adopting a threshold of $1,000, or $1 million, per QALY.

The reality is that there are methods for putting an explicit dollar value on life. Chapter 8 describes how to do it.

ENDNOTES

1. A. Gore, 1990, "Is Oregon's Health-Care Plan a Bold Experiment or a Poor Man's Burden?" *Los Angeles Times* 30 May 1990 sec. B, p. 7.

2. D. Fox and H. Leichter, 1991, "Rationing in Oregon: The New Accountability," *Health Affairs* 10(3): 7–27.

3. Some readers may note that because the demand for organs outstrips the supply, access to transplants is already rationed. Oregon further restricted access based on ability to pay.

4. M. Specter, "Rising Cost of Medical Treatment Forces Oregon to 'Play God,'" *Washington Post* 5 February 1988, p. A1.

5. A. Japenga, "A Transplant for Coby," Los Angeles Times 5 December 1987, pt. 5, p. 1. Note that prenatal care was never mentioned during the initial debate on transplant funding.

6. Fox and Leichter, ibid.

7. Ibid.

8. Ibid.

9. Economists will note that this argument is only partially correct. The decision not to cover individuals is not rationing per se, but it leads to price rationing if those individuals cannot otherwise afford medical care.

10. L. Rein, "N.J. May Soon Face Health Care Rationing," Bergen Record 29 April 1991, p. A3.

11. Gore, ibid.

12. T. Egan, "New Health Test: The Oregon Plan," The New York Times 6 May 1990, sec. 1, p. 31.

13. T. Egan, "Oregon Lists Illnesses by Priority to See Who Gets Medicaid Care," *The New York Times* 2 May 1990, sec. A, p. 1.

14. "A Brave Medical Experiment Cuts Costs at the Expense of the Poor," *The New York Times* 22 May 1990, sec. A, p. 26.

15. V. Morell, 1990, "Oregon Puts Bold Health Plan on Ice," *Science* 3 August 1990, p. 468.

16. Fox and Leichter, ibid.

17. Physicians who commented on the list made similar observations. See T. Bodenheimer, 1997, p. 655.

18. Condition-treatment rankings can move up and down over time. This is why pair 566 in 1991 is different from pair 566 in 2002.

19. Quoted in R. Knox, "With Revised Plan, Oregon Pursues Medicaid Rationing," *Boston Globe* 21 May 1991, p. 4.

20. Quoted in S. Russell, 1992, "AIDS Activists Split on Oregon Health Plan," *San Francisco Chronicle* 27 April 1992, p. A4.

21. L. Brown, 1991, "The National Politics of Oregon's Rationing Plan," *Health Affairs* 10(3): 37.

22. Ibid.

23. Ibid, pp. 36–37.

24. T. Bodenheimer, 1997, "The Oregon Health Plan—Lessons for the Nation," *New England Journal of Medicine* 337(9): 651–55.

25. R. Kaplan, "Utility Assessment for Estimating Quality Adjusted Life Years," in F. Sloan, ed., *Valuing Health Care,* Cambridge: Cambridge University Press. p. 59.

26. Bodenheimer, ibid.

27. Quoted in P. Kilborn, "Oregon Falters on a New Path to Health Care," *The New York Times* 3 January 1999, sec. 1, p. 1.

28. For example, see P. Kilborn, 1999, and N. Timmins, 2000, "Oregon Grapples with Healthcare Plan," *Financial Times* 26 April 2000, p. 5.

29. Quoted in A. Schrader, "Panel Seeks Health Debate," *Denver Post* 7 November 1998, p. A1.

8 WHAT IS YOUR LIFE WORTH?

In March 2002, the U.S. government issued guidelines for compensating the next of kin of the victims of the September 11, 2001, terrorist attacks. The government divided compensation into two parts—an economic component based on the victim's income-earning potential, and a noneconomic component. Due to the large number of young professionals who perished in the attacks, the average economic component amounted to $1.6 million. This dwarfed the noneconomic component, which was set at $250,000. The idea that the value of a life lost in the September 11 tragedies was almost entirely dependent on the victim's earnings did not sit well with many individuals. One woman, whose mother died in the World Trade Center attack, understood that the United States was saying that "the value of a life is $250,000."[1]

There is no getting around the fact that the U.S. government had put a price on life. It could hardly be faulted for tackling this difficult issue—the public demanded that the next of kin receive some form of compensation for their loss. What may be surprising is that this is hardly the first time the U.S. government has put a price on life. Nor is the U.S. government alone in attempting to do this. Many health services researchers, academics, and even private citizens have also attempted to determine how much a life is worth. Their estimates range from less than $250,000 to more than $5 million.

As payers inch closer to using such values as a basis for rationing health care, our access to services may depend on which number they use. With such a big potential range of values to choose from, it is important that they get it right.

WILLINGNESS TO PAY, HUMAN CAPITAL, AND INTRINSIC VALUE

The U.S. government's approach to valuing life in the aftermath of September 11 was based on seminal research published three decades earlier by economist Michael Grossman.[2] Describing the "demand for health," Grossman suggested that we could put a price on health in much the same way as we put a price on consumer goods. When it comes to pricing consumer goods, the experts are market researchers. To determine the price to set for a consumer good like a DVD player, marketers use the concept of *willingness to pay* (WTP). The WTP for a DVD player equals the dollar amount of other goods and services that people are willing to give up to obtain the DVD player.

Marketers use surveys to determine the WTP for DVD players. The surveys are rather simple, often reducing to a simple question: "How much are you willing to pay for a DVD player?" If most people say they are willing to pay at least $200 for a DVD player, this means that they are willing to give up $200 worth of other goods to buy it. This is not some ivory-tower concept; if they make the purchase, they really will have $200 less to spend on other stuff. Given such consumer preferences, the DVD manufacturer can confidently set a price at $200, anticipating that consumers will gladly pay it.

Grossman extends the idea to health. He agrees with Victor Fuchs' compelling argument—presented in Chapter 1—that dollars spent on health care must come at the expense of other valuable goods and services. Thus, it is reasonable to ask people how much they are willing to pay to improve their health, and it is reasonable to expect some answer other than "an infinite amount." However, we should expect the WTP for improving health to exceed the WTP for most other goods and services. After all, most people hold their health more dearly than products like DVD players.

This conclusion raises a very important question: Why are people willing to pay so much to be healthy? Some people may be willing to pay a considerable amount for other goods and services, such as DVD players, because they believe that buying and owning stuff will make them happy. By the same token, must of us are willing to pay a lot for our health because we believe that being healthy will make us happy. After all, good health allows us to eat at nice restaurants,, walk through a forest, watch movies, and do most everything else that we enjoy. Economists sometimes refer to this "happiness factor" as the *intrinsic value of health*. This is what the U.S. government called the noneconomic component in the September 11 compensation package.

Grossman points out another reason most people are willing to pay so much to be healthy. Being healthy enables people to work harder so that they can make more money and purchase more of the other things that make them happy. Grossman calls this the *human capital value* of health. The term *human capital* reflects the idea that, like other business capital, our health contributes toward our productivity. Education is another important source of human capital. Goods like a DVD player, however, are not likely to contribute much to someone's human capital (unless the consumer is studying to be a filmmaker).

According to Grossman's framework, the dollar value of health is the sum of its intrinsic value and human capital value. The September 11 compensation plan reflects this idea. The United States offered $250,000 in compensation for the intrinsic value of life, and anywhere from zero to several million dollars for the human capital component. This fact raises two other important questions: Is $250,000 a reasonable estimate of the intrinsic value of life? Is the intrinsic value the same for everyone?

In recent years, economists have made extensive use of the WTP approach to estimate both the human capital and intrinsic components of the value of a life. But economists are not the only ones who have put a price on life. Juries and the U.S. National Institutes of Health (NIH), among others, have also done it. Before examining their methods, take a moment to ponder the following question.

> Suppose you could put a dollar value on your life. Without specifying an exact amount, which component would be higher—your human capital or the intrinsic value of your life? _____

I have asked this question of many individuals. Most agree that the intrinsic value of their lives greatly exceeds their human capital. The occasional exceptions are MBA students who expect to earn several million dollars in their lifetimes. Bear this in mind as we consider various alternatives for putting a price on life.

PRICING LIFE IN THE REAL WORLD

Every day, ordinary people in the United States put a dollar value on life and limb. They are jurors in civil lawsuits in which an individual or firm is accused of negligently causing injury or death. If a defendant is found to be negligent, the jury must calculate a cash award to compensate the victim or next of kin. The purpose of the compensation award is twofold: to make the victim whole (or to make the next of kin whole), and to deter negligence. The logic behind deterrence is that if individuals know they will be forced to pay the full cost of their bad acts, they will take an appropriate measure of caution.

The compensation award usually has two major parts. First, it should include any medical costs resulting from the negligence. This can be quite a substantial sum—the lifetime medical costs for an infant injured at birth can run into the millions of dollars. But this amount should not be confused with the value of a life. To see why not, imagine that someone negligently kills two people. One victim one dies instantly and costlessly, while the other survives for a full year in a costly coma. Although the jury award would probably be greater in the latter case, this would not mean that the latter victim's life was more valuable than the life of the former victim.

The next of kin of the victim who died instantaneously would not necessarily walk away from a trial penniless. Juries also consider the victim's income-earning potential—that is, the human capital component of the value of a life. There is a rather perverse message in this. If you are going to negligently kill someone, you will be far better off financially if you kill an elderly homeless individual than if you kill Cameron Diaz or Kobe Bryant.

Apart from medical costs and lost wages, juries are not required to consider any other factors when making an award. Juries sometimes include an amount for pain and suffering or loss of consortium, but if the victim lived alone and did not suffer, then these amounts are nil. Juries may also award punitive damages in the case of particularly egregious conduct, but this payment is meant as a deterrent rather than as compensation for the loss. Put it all together, and this means that the value of life as computed by a jury largely reflects the deceased's human capital. In failing to account for the intrinsic value of life, juries awards may drastically understate the value of life, and therefore fail to provide sufficient deterrence to negligence.

THE COST-OF-ILLNESS (COI) APPROACH

As health care costs began to mount in the 1960s and 1970s, public health advocates tried to persuade government officials and taxpayers that it was worth spending additional money to prevent disease. They argued that spending for medical research and public health improvements was dwarfed by the cost of illness (COI). In 2000, the U.S. Congress Joint Economic Committee (JEC) calculated that the national COI exceeded $3 trillion annually and lamented that the NIH, the world's leading funder of basic research on disease and prevention, had a budget of merely $16 billion to fight "this $3 trillion battle."[3]

The JEC made classic cost-benefit arguments in favor of increasing the NIH budget. For example, the committee claimed that $70 million spent for research on testicular cancer reduced the COI from that disease by $180 million annually, and a $180 laser treatment for blindness saved $1.5 billion annually. The arguments worked—Congress enacted a plan to double NIH funding over a five-year period.

Advocates of COI methods use them as a benchmark for valuing health care spending. Does this mean that the COI is a useful measure of the value of a life? The COI methodology for valuing life is similar to the approach used by juries, with the same two key components.[4] The *direct COI* consists of medical costs. The *indirect COI* consists of lost human capital. Of the roughly $3 trillion annual COI in the United States in the year 2000, the direct costs represented about $1.3 trillion and human capital costs about $1.7 billion.[5] The diseases with the highest COI tend to be those with the highest incidence, including heart disease, cancer, and diabetes.[6] If we take the annual COI for an illness like cardiovascular disease (nearly $300 billion) and divide that figure by the number of individuals who die from it, we get a *cost-per-lost-life* of about $200,000. Of course, some of the COI was for individuals who got sick but did not die, so the actual cost-per-lost-life is less than this amount. Even so, we will use $200,000 as the COI benchmark measure of the value of a life, though in reality the figure is somewhat lower.

As with jury awards, the COI is a flawed measure because it omits the intrinsic value of life. The NIH acknowledges that its estimates of COI do not include "some important aspects of the burden of illness," such as pain and suffering and the "deterioration ... in quality of life."[7] Some important aspects indeed—for most people, the deterioration of the quality of life would probably be the most important aspect. Thus far, the NIH has shied away from putting a dollar value on this intrinsic component. This is a shame, because the NIH uses COI measures to justify medical research and public health spending. By excluding the intrinsic component, the NIH understates the benefits of medical spending.

USING SURVEYS TO PUT A PRICE ON GOOD HEALTH

Through surveys, focus groups, and other research tools, marketers determine how much consumers are willing to pay for goods ranging from automobiles to restaurant meals. In the last two decades, health services researchers have applied the same market research tools to estimate the WTP for good health. Some of this work has even made its way into practical use.

The U.S. Environmental Protection Agency (EPA) has been an important proponent of WTP methods. The EPA often requires businesses to incur considerable expenses to reduce pollution. To justify these requirements, the EPA sometimes uses cost-benefit analysis. EPA data show convincingly that cleaner air and water translate into better health. The EPA combines these data with WTP measures to put a dollar value on the health benefits.

To do this, the EPA needs valid WTP measures. In a well-documented effort from the 1980s, the EPA asked researchers at the University of Chicago to measure the WTP to avoid several minor symptoms of air pollution. The research team, led by Robert Fabian and George Tolley, took an approach that was based in market research.[8] They identified a sample of respondents to be interviewed. The interviewer handed each respondent a card describing a symptom, such as sinus problems or nausea. The description of sinus problems might read like this.

Sinus Problems: You will have congestion and pain in your sinuses and forehead all day. You will be bothered by a feeling of stuffiness in your head. You will need to blow your nose every few minutes. You will have to breathe through your mouth most of the time.

Next, the interviewer asked respondents to consider how their households normally spend their income. This instruction helped to point out the trade-offs involved in spending more money on health care. Then, the interviewer would get to the nub of the matter:

If your health symptoms in the next 12 months were the same as in the last 12 months, except that you would be faced with one additional day of sinus problems, would it be worth *$100* to you to completely get rid of this day of symptoms?

The interviewer would repeat this question, varying the cash amount until the respondent reached the point of indifference between spending the money and enduring the symptom. The corresponding dollar amount is the respondent's WTP to avoid one day of sinus problems.

You can think about the same question. What is your willingness to pay to avoid one day of sinus problems? Fill in your answer below.

Willingness to pay to avoid one day of sinus problems:

_____

Here are descriptions of symptoms for drowsiness and nausea. After each, jot down your WTP to avoid one day of these symptoms.

Drowsiness: You will have extreme difficulty staying awake during 6 of the hours when you are normally awake. You will doze off for an instant now and then. The drowsiness will interfere with your normal activities.

Willingness to pay to avoid one day of drowsiness:

_____

Nausea: Throughout the day, you will have a lingering urge to vomit, but you will not be able to do so. Stomach distress will be strong. There will be no actual pain.

Willingness to pay to avoid one day of nausea:

_____

The actual survey research is more meticulous, of course. Researchers make sure that responses are consistent with other information obtained during the interview. For example, if individuals state during their interview that they dread nausea more than other symptoms, then their WTP for avoiding nausea should be higher than for other symptoms. Researchers also tell respondents not to take into account the availability of inexpensive remedies from the drug store. This way, respondents think only about the value of health, and not about the cheapest ways to stay healthy.

SOME WTP MEASURES

Robert Fabian and George Tolley reported WTP measures they obtained in their EPA-sponsored research. Their data are from the 1980s, so I have adjusted their findings for inflation. Table 8.1 provides a sampling of their adjusted WTP scores.

TABLE 8.1 Willingness to Pay to Avoid Symptoms: Results from a Survey[y]

SYMPTOM	AVOIDANCE PAYMENT
Coughing	$42
Drowsiness	$45
Headaches	$60
Nausea	$75
Sinus problems	$50

How did your responses compare? Do not be surprised if your responses differ considerably from those reported in Table 8.1. Fabian and Tolley found considerable variation in WTP from one respondent to the next.[10] It would not be unusual for one person to report a WTP to avoid one day of headaches of $30 and the next respondent to report a WTP of $90. Responses above $200 would be quite rare, however.

Variation in responses could reflect differences in how individuals interpret these rather unusual survey questions. Not everyone will imagine the symptoms of a headache in exactly the same way. But some of the variation reflects genuine differences in how individuals trade off money and health. If your answers are consistently higher than those reported by Fabian and Tolley, then you probably place a relatively higher price on your health than do most other people. One might expect wealthier individuals to have higher WTP, but Fabian and Tolley found little evidence of this. Nor did the respondent's medical history affect WTP.

WILLINGNESS TO PAY FOR LIFE

Researchers have used the same techniques to measure the value of life, or, more precisely, the value of a life-year. To measure the WTP for a year of life, a researcher might pose the following scenario (you can fill in your answer at the end).[11] Read it carefully, since it asks about something you have probably never had to think about.

> Based on current epidemiological data, you can expect to live until age 80. One of the major risks of death that you will face is stroke. You currently have a 10 percent lifetime chance of dying from a stroke. If you can avoid dying from stroke, your life expectancy will increase by 2 years, to age 82. How much would you be willing to pay to devise programs that would reduce your chances of a stroke by 5 percentage points, from 10 percent to 5 percent? (Note that another way to say this is that your risk of stroke would drop 50 percent.) _____

You can use your response to the stroke question to compute your WTP for a life-year. The expected gain in longevity from the stroke reduction programs is 0.1 years.[12] Thus, to obtain your WTP for a full year of life, you need to multiply

your response by 10. Enter this amount here: _____.
Remember, this is your WTP for a full year of life.

For most people, their response to the stroke question
depends on their age. A young person may place relatively little value on living a few extra years beyond age 80 because the
benefits are very remote. A person who is approaching age 80
will probably value those extra years very highly. To compute
WTP values that are independent of age, it is necessary to
apply a multiplier that is related to the discount factor discussed in Chapter 5. In the calculations that follow, I assume a
discount rate of 5 percent.

Table 8.2 allows you to determine your "age-adjusted"
WTP for a year of life. Find your current age (or the closest age
to your current age) in column 1. Enter your WTP for a full
year of life, based on your response to the stroke question, in
the appropriate row of column 2. Multiply by the adjustment
factor in column 3 and enter the resulting amount in column
4. The result is your *age-adjusted WTP for a year of life*.
Remember this amount. You will need it later on when you
compute how much your life is worth.

TABLE 8.2   Computing Your Age-Adjusted Value of a Life-Year

(1) YOUR AGE	(2) WTP FOR A FULL YEAR OF LIFE	(3) MULTIPLICATION FACTOR	(4) AGE-ADJUSTED WTP FOR A YEAR OF LIFE
75		1.3	
65		2.0	
55		3.5	
45		5.5	
35		9.0	

A team of researchers at the University of Michigan
recently reviewed over half a dozen WTP measures obtained
using methods like these.[13] The median age-adjusted WTP for
a year of healthy life was $160,000.

How Useful Are WTP Measures?

There are many reasons to be skeptical about using surveys to put a dollar value on good health. For one thing, respondents must be reasonably adept at working with probabilities. To aid respondents in this regard, survey researchers often use a probability wheel like the one described in Chapter 6. Another problem is that some survey responses make no sense. Fabian and Tolley admit that some respondents to their survey bid zero. Taken literally, this means the respondents were unwilling to pay anything, not even 25 cents, to avoid a daylong headache or a day of nausea. There are not enough masochists to explain the large number of zero responses, and we can only wonder about their true WTP. Other respondents reported unrealistically high WTP amounts (often approaching their annual incomes!). These unlikely responses put Fabian and Tolley in the uncomfortable position of having to decide which responses to keep and which to throw out.

Survey researchers have found other troubling oddities in WTP studies. Studies consistently show that many respondents are willing to pay only a small amount to avoid a symptom, yet insist on receiving a king's ransom to endure the same symptom. (For example, a respondent might be willing to pay no more than $50 to avoid a headache but would be unwilling to suffer a headache unless paid at least $1,000.) This is known as the *framing problem*. Individuals also seem willing to pay an extraordinary premium to eliminate the last shred of risk of falling ill. Thus, an individual who might be willing to pay $50 to reduce the number of annual headaches from two to one might be willing to pay an extra $250 to reduce the number from one to zero. This is known as the *certainty premium*. Both the framing problem and the certainty premium suggest that researchers can manipulate WTP findings to an extent by carefully wording the questions.

STATISTICAL VERSUS IDENTIFIED LIVES

In most WTP surveys about valuing life-years, the scenarios involve some small probability that the individual's health will be affected. This makes sense when trying to value the benefits of biomedical research or public health programs, where respondents know that everyone has a statistical probability of reaping the benefits. Researchers say that responses to these surveys provide valid information about the value of *statistical lives*. Surveyors rarely ask questions like this one:

Suppose that a loved one will die from kidney failure unless he or she undergoes dialysis. How much are you willing to pay for the dialysis treatment?

The response to this life-or-death question may be more pertinent when evaluating health care services targeting identifiable individuals. The responses would provide information about the value of *identified lives*.

There is no reason to expect that the value of a statistical life would equal the value of an identified life. However, it is possible to conjecture which one is larger. Recall the massive fund raising efforts in Oregon to pay for Coby Howard's transplant operation. There are countless other examples like this. What frustrated John Kitzhaber was that the same money, spent on public health programs, could have saved many more lives. The fact that the public was willing to spend so extravagantly on just one individual suggests that the WTP for identified lives exceeds the WTP for statistical lives.

THE ECONOMIC APPROACH TO VALUING STATISTICAL LIVES

Market researchers know that surveys are not always reliable. Sometimes, people do not respond truthfully, and they may even try to manipulate survey results. At other times, survey respondents give what they think is an honest response, but they balk when the time comes to put their money where their mouth is. Consider market research on DVD players. Some respondents might think that if they report a low WTP for a DVD player, the DVD manufacturer will set a lower price. Or, they might report a WTP of $200, believing that this is the amount they really would be willing to pay, yet balk when it comes time to actually make the purchase. For this reason, market researchers pay attention to what people actually buy, and not just what they say they will buy.

The same arguments apply to valuing health. A retiree might report an extremely high WTP for stroke prevention, hoping that this will boost government spending on stroke research, with funding coming from other people's taxes. Another individual might tell a survey researcher that WTP for a statistical year of life is $100,000, yet hesitate when asked to spend $10,000 for a procedure that has 10 percent chance of adding 1 year in life expectancy (which works out to an expense of $100,000 per life-year). To nail down the WTP for a statistical life, researchers ought to observe real-world behavior and not just rely on surveys.

The thought of observing real-world purchases of life-years seems rather absurd. It is not as if there is some store called "Years, Lives, and Beyond" where consumers can purchase a chance to live an extra year. Nor do people visit their doctors to explicitly purchase life-years. (Patient: "Doc, how much do you charge for 5 QALYs?" Doctor: "Huh?") But some individuals do make explicit trade-offs between dollars and statistical life-years. In particular, workers who take on risky jobs often insist on receiving higher pay. Economists have exploited this trade-off between job risks and wages to compute a "real-world" value of a statistical life.

People do not always insist on getting paid to risk their lives. People go to war for their countries out of a sense of duty and patriotism. But the history of warfare teaches us that even patriotism has its limits. On many occasions, warriors will not do battle without a promise of financial reward. In 1415, King Henry V of England hoped to conquer Northern France and force a marriage to Princess Catherine, the daughter of French

King Charles VI. He asked his nobility to join his quest. As told in the famous Laurence Olivier movie production of Shakespeare's play (released during World War II), the noblemen supported Henry for the glory of England.

According to historian John Keegan, the movie's spin on the Battle of Agincourt was mainly propaganda.[14] Medieval fighting was dangerous, and few noblemen would risk their lives for their country. However, they would risk their lives for money. A nobleman's goal was not to kill the enemy but to capture him and hold him hostage until ransomed. As Keegan tells it, the English nobility were on the verge of a fabulously profitable campaign near the Normandy town of Agincourt when an onrush of French knights forced Henry to order the execution of hostages. Denied the spoils of their battle, the noblemen turned against their King.

History provides many other examples in which people took great risks in exchange for the promise of great financial rewards. During the age of oceangoing exploration, captains like Columbus and Magellan promised their sailors a share of any treasures they might discover. Napoleon assembled an army to conquer Egypt by promising each man a plot of land upon a successful return.

Today, we see the same types of trade-offs between money and risk at dangerous work sites. Construction workers are paid more to build the fiftieth floor of an office building than to build the first floor. Chemical workers receive a premium to work with hazardous materials. There are countless other examples. Assuming that employers do not pay extra wages out of the goodness of their hearts, we must conclude that they are forced to pay higher wages to get workers to take these risky jobs. In other words, the wage premium represents the amount that workers insist on receiving to take on an extra risk to life and limb.

If this logic is correct, then it is possible to estimate the value of a statistical life by measuring the relationship between wages and job risk. For example, suppose that the wage for a job with a 2-in-1,000 risk of a work-related fatality is $50,000, and the wage for a similar job with a 3-in-1,000 risk is $52,000. This implies that each worker must be compensated $2,000 to take on an additional 1-in-1,000 risk of death. If 1,000 workers take on the risky job, they will collectively receive an extra $2 million in compensation, but they face the expectation of one extra fatality. This puts the value of a statistical life at $2 million.

This example illustrates the basic technique used by economists to estimate the value of a statistical life. They collect data on wages and job risks for millions of workers and determine the trade-off between the two. Wages can vary for many reasons besides job risk, of course, so researchers performing these studies must control for as many of these factors as possible. Richard Thaler and Sherwin Rosen published the first such study in 1976.[15] They found that the value of a statistical life was about $1 million (in 2002 dollars). There have been dozens of studies since 1975. W. Kip Viscusi has used highly detailed data on wages and job risk, and his studies suggest that the value of a statistical life is more like $5 million.[16] Other studies put the figure as high as $20 million. Given the average life expectancy of the workers who were studied, and using a discount rate of 5 percent, the $5 million estimate works out to a value of a life-year of about $300,000. (The value of a life-year would be a bit smaller if we used a smaller discount rate.) Other studies put the value of a statistical life-year between $200,000 and $300,000.

Some critics of these studies question whether workers know the risks involved in dangerous jobs. Workers must know the jobs are dangerous, or else they would not insist on higher wages. Many workers have quite good information about the risks they face. Unions do a good job of providing information about job risks. Some workers in risky jobs have advanced degrees in fields like chemistry and also seem likely to have good information about job risk.

Even if many workers lack good information, this does not invalidate Viscusi's finding that a statistical life is worth $5 million. Suppose that workers systematically underestimate risks (perhaps believing that they are largely immune from the risks that face others). Or suppose that workers underestimate the range of risks from one job to another, incorrectly believing that most jobs are about equally risky. In either case, some complex economic theory reveals that the value of a statistical life would be at least $5 million. Remember that the value of an identified life is even higher. No matter how you slice it, economic studies suggest that the value of a life is very high indeed!

OTHER EVIDENCE ON THE VALUE OF LIFE

Economists have also studied risky decisions outside the job. Whether buying a house in a polluted area, failing to install a smoke detector, not wearing seat belts, or driving too fast for road conditions, individuals routinely take risks to life and limb in return for extra money or extra time (which, itself, has a dollar value). A recent review of these studies pegs the dollar value of a statistical life at somewhere between $1 million and $6 million.[17] A statistical life-year is worth between $100,000 and $300,000.

Of course, the gold standard for WTP studies would be to examine patient expenditures for medical care. Due to the prevalence of health insurance, it is difficult to find situations where consumers pay full out-of-pocket prices for medical care. However, one recent study does provide direct evidence on WTP.[18] This study finds that low dose aspirin therapy—a mainstay of baby boomers trying to prevent heart disease—costs $150,000 per year of life saved.

What is striking about this study is how well the $150,000 figure conforms with findings in other studies. It is easy for critics to second-guess one or two studies on claims that consumers lack information or do not behave rationally. How then to explain the consistency of the research findings? Either consumers are always uninformed and irrational in the same way, or there is a valid methodology in this madness.

Of course, the fact that the average person pegs the value of a statistical life-year at around $150,000 does not imply that this figure holds for everyone. Each of us makes trade-offs between health and other goods and services. A year of life may be worth much more to you, or much less, than $150,000.

WHAT IS YOUR LIFE WORTH?

Payers have several options for valuing life. The COI approach gives the most conservative valuations because it ignores the intrinsic value of life. Using the COI approach, the value of a life varies from one person to the next, because incomes vary. To determine the value of your own life using NIH methods, you need to compute the discounted value of your own lifetime income.

Table 8.3 gives the approximate value of life for someone between the ages of 25 and 65 who has $10,000 in annual earnings.[19] To figure out the human capital value of your life, just divide your annual income by $10,000, and multiply by the appropriate figure in the table. For example, if you are 45 years old and earn $80,000 annually, the human capital value of your life equals 8 times $150,000, or $1.2 million.

TABLE 8.3   The Human Capital Value of Your Life

YOUR AGE	VALUE OF YOUR LIFE PER $10,000 IN ANNUAL EARNINGS
65	$0 (assumes you are retired)
55	$85,000
45	$150,000
35	$190,000
25	$225,000

WTP surveys report values of statistical life-years. Given a respondent's life expectancy, it is possible to translate these values into a WTP for a life. You can use your response to the stroke question to compute your WTP for your own life (in the statistical sense, of course). Using Table 8.4, enter your age-adjusted WTP for a year of life in the appropriate row of column 2. Multiply this value by the figure in column 3, and put the result in column 4; this is your value for a statistical life. This calculation assumes that you can expect to live to age 80.

TABLE 8.4 Your WTP for a Statistical Life

(1) YOUR AGE	(2) YOUR AGE-ADJUSTED WTP FOR A YEAR OF LIFE	(3) MULTIPLICATION FACTOR	(4) YOUR VALUE FOR A LIFE
75		4	
65		10	
55		14	
45		17	
35		18	

The typical age-adjusted WTP for a year of life is about $150,000. For someone age 45, this translates into a WTP for a statistical life of about $2.5 million. How did you compare? Do you hold your life dearer than most?

Labor market studies like Viscusi's provide a value of life for the average respondent that is about twice the value of life obtained from WTP surveys. But it is impossible to determine your own preference for life versus wages without observing your real-world behavior.

VALUE OF A QALY

Survey methods ask respondents to consider their WTP to avoid an unexpected death. Most respondents are healthy, so the comparison they make is between death and full health. Thus, the reported WTP for a year of life is a good measure of the WTP for a QALY. If we believe the survey evidence or the labor market studies, then the WTP for a QALY is at least $150,000, and perhaps twice that high.

It is interesting to compare the $150,000 figure against the previously reported amounts that survey respondents were willing to pay to avoid one day of illness. For example, recall that the WTP to avoid one day of headaches is about $50. The QALY score for headaches is about 0.8, so $50 buys a one-day improvement of 0.2 QALYs. On an annual basis, this works out to about $90,000 per QALY, which is in the same ballpark.

Regardless of which number is correct, the data all point to the same important conclusion: The cost-effectiveness thresholds used by NICE, Australia's PBS, Canada, and other government payers are too low. NICE has refused to pay for interventions that cost more than £30,000 (about $45,000) per QALY. The rule of thumb in Canada is to refuse coverage if the cost per QALY exceeds $60,000 (in U.S. dollars). It seems that most people think that life is worth a lot more than their governments are willing to pay.

RESPONDING TO MR. MORTIMER

Jim Mortimer, the president of the Midwest Business Group on Health, was speaking for many people when he opined that new medical technologies were not worth the cost. No one can deny that new medical technologies are a major cause of rising medical costs. Nor can anyone deny that new medical technologies are a major reason for continuing improvements in life expectancy and the quality of life. To determine whether the financial costs outweigh the medical benefits, one must be able to place both costs and health on a common scale. We now have that scale—we can put a dollar value on life.

In a series of studies with various colleagues, economist David Cutler has put Mr. Mortimer's claim to the test.[20] In one study, Cutler and Mark McClellan measured the health benefits of several new medical technologies, put a dollar value on these benefits, and compared this value with the associated costs. For example, they found that new technologies have driven up the cost of treating heart attacks by an average of $10,000 since 1984. These same technologies have increased the life expectancy of heart attack victims by 1 year. Using a conservative value of a life-year of $100,000, and adjusting for discounting, they estimate that new technologies have created a benefit of $70,000.[21] Using similar methods, they find that technological change drove up the cost of treating low-birth-weight babies by $40,000 between 1950 and 1990. But life expectancies for these neonates increased by 12 years, generating a benefit of $240,000 (after discounting). For these and most other conditions studied by Cutler and McClellan, the benefits of technological change exceed the costs.

In an even more ambitious study, Cutler and Elizabeth Richardson computed the expected number of QALYS that an average person can expect to enjoy from birth to death.[22] One could call this a "QALY expectancy," because it is like a life expectancy but adjusts for the quality of life. Using a value per QALY of $100,000 and adjusting for discounting, they put a dollar value on the typical American's QALY expectancy. We can call this the DVQALY for short. They found that a baby born in 1970 had a DVQALY of $2.35 million. For a baby born in 1990, the DVQALY rose to about $2.44 million, an increase of $99,000. In comparison, expected lifetime medical costs rose by only $19,000. Even if half the increase in DVQALY is due to factors other than medical care (such as lifestyle), the benefit/cost ratio is still very favorable.

THE BOTTOM LINE

Anyone who wants to seriously argue that the benefits of medical technology are not worth the cost must eventually put a dollar value on health. This is true whether the critic is an employer balking at paying health benefits or a government agency balking at raising taxes to pay for new therapies. The question is, therefore, not whether we should take on the challenge of putting a price on life, but how we should do it. Economists, health services researchers, and public health officials have advocated a variety of approaches. Depending on the methodology, the value of a life ranges from less than $200,000 to $5 million or more. Smaller values are based on methods that ignore or minimize the intrinsic value of life. But surveys and evidence from real-world behavior confirm that most people hold their lives dear and place a very high value on the intrinsic value.

Though many people like to complain about rising health care costs, any reasonable cost/benefit analysis would conclude that we are getting our money's worth. This does not mean that public and private payers cannot do a better job of assuring that health dollars are well spent. In Chapter 9, I describe the imperative to control health care spending and discuss the prospects for using rational rationing to make sure we get our money's worth.

ENDNOTES

1. Quoted in F. James, "Revised Payout Package Draws Ire," *Chicago Tribune* 9 March 2002, p. 1.

2. M. Grossman, 1972, "On the Concept of Health Capital and the Demand for Health," *Journal of Political Economy* 80: 223–55.

3. Joint Economic Committee reports quoted in M. Kondrake, 2000, "Investing Billions in Health Research Can Save Trillions," *Roll Call* 25 May 2000.

4. For example, see D. Rice, 1966, *Estimating the Cost of Illness* Health Economics ser no. 6, Washington, DC: U.S. Department of Health, Education and Welfare, Public Health Service.

5. These figures are taken from H. Varmus, 1997, "Disease-Specific Estimates of Direct and Indirect Costs of Illness and NIH Support," U.S. Department of Health and Human Services, National Institutes of Health, and updated for inflation.

6. There are potential flaws in disease-specific measures. See D. Kenkel, 1994, "Cost of Illness Approach," in G. Tolley, D. Kenkel, and R. Fabian, eds., *Valuing Health for Policy,* Chicago: University of Chicago Press.

7. Varmus, ibid.

8. For more details, see R. Fabian and G. Tolley, 1994, "Issues in Questionnaire Design," in Tolley et al., *Valuing Health for Policy,* Chicago: University of Chicago Press.

9. See M. Brien, D. Kenkel, A. Kelly, and R. Fabian, 1994, "Empirical Results from Household Personal Interviews," in Tolley et al., *Valuing Health for Policy,* Chicago: University of Chicago Press, p. 172. Copyright 1994 by the University of Chicago.

10. In statistical parlance, the standard deviations of responses exceeded the means.

11. This is loosely based on a question in R. Fabian et al., "Design of Contingent Valuation Approaches to Serious Illness," in Tolley, Kenkel, and Fabian.

12. This is because (1) 5 percent of patients will benefit from the programs, and (2), the benefit will last 2 years, on average. Multiplying together, this gives an expected benefit of 0.1 years.

13. R. Hirth et al., 2000, "Willingness to Pay for a Quality-Adjusted Life Year," *Medical Decision Making* 20(3): 332–42.

14. J. Keegan, 1976, *The Face of Battle,* New York: Penguin.

15. R. Thaler and S. Rosen, 1976, "The Value of Saving a Life: Evidence from the Labor Market," in N. Terleckyz, ed., *Household Production and Consumption*, New York: Columbia University Press.

16. A good job of summarizing this literature appears in W.K. Viscusi, 1992, *Fatal Tradeoffs,* New York: Oxford University Press.

17. Hirth et al., ibid.

18. U. Ladabaum et al., 2001, "Aspirin as an Adjunct to Screening for Prevention of Sporadic Colorectal Cancer," *Annals of Internal Medicine* 135(9): 769–81.

19. To make these calculations, I assume that earnings will increase 2 percent annually and that the retirement age is 65. As always in this chapter, I use a discount rate of 5 percent.

20. Either individually, together, or with various other authors, they have published numerous studies. Perhaps their best known is D. Cutler and M. McClellan, 2001, "Is Technological Change in Medicine Worth It?" *Health Affairs* 20(5): 11–29.

21. They also allow for future costs (recall the discussion in Chapter 5).

22. D. Cutler and L. Richardson, 1999, "Your Money and Your Life: The Value of Health and What Affects It," in A. Garber, ed., *Frontiers in Health Policy Research*, Cambridge, MA: MIT Press, pp. 99–132.

9 RISING COSTS AND RATIONAL RATIONING

Nearly 2,500 years ago, Hippocrates said "health is the greatest of blessings." Surveys and labor market studies provide numbers to support this aphorism. Our lives are so dear—at least $150,000 per QALY—that most every health care intervention, from vaccinations to transplants, produces aggregate benefits that outweigh the total costs. Indeed, one of the key lessons from the Tammy Tengs study described in Chapter 2 is that health care interventions tend to be far more cost effective than other life-saving interventions, including pollution control and job safety improvements. Of the 310 health care interventions that Tengs studied, only 41 exceeded the $150,000 threshold. Compare this across-the-board cost-effectiveness with other popular life-saving interventions, such as asbestos control ($5 million or more per life year saved) or seat belts for school bus passengers (nearly $3 million per life year saved). Whether weighed against the absolute value of life, or against other life-saving interventions, health care is almost always a good buy.

Yet those who foot the bill do not see it this way, and question the wisdom of spending even more on health care. Citing the theories of moral hazard, demand inducement, and practice variations—to the extent they cite any theories at all—payers claim that there is too much inefficient health care spending, and they are doing what they can to hold the line.

Payers are correct in that much health care spending is inefficient. Not everyone who receives costly medical care really needs it, even if the average patient has much to gain. Copayments, capitation, and utilization controls all have a role in eliminating waste. However, these cost containment strategies have not prevented health care costs from increasing. Payers seem intent on halting any further growth in health spending.

Focusing on the bottom line ignores benefit–cost trade-offs, which makes no sense. The best available evidence shows that increases in health care spending are producing remarkable improvements in longevity and quality of life. Using economic estimates of the value of health, the benefits of new technologies often exceed the costs by a ratio of 5 to 1 or more. We hold our lives dear; it seems that those who want to stop health care spending in its tracks do not.

Patients around the world know the importance of accessing the best technologies and best trained providers that medicine has to offer. Caught in payers' frenetic efforts to keep spending under control, patients are becoming increasingly frustrated with bureaucratic red tape in the United States, lengthening queues in England and Canada, copayments in France, complex physician regulations in Germany, and needless delays in obtaining new drugs everywhere. If recent trends continue, this misplaced focus is likely to cause even more suffering for patients in the years ahead.

THE HEALTH CARE BUDGET "CRISIS"

Health care spending has been increasing steadily for decades. During the 1970s and 1980s, payers adopted a variety of cost containment strategies with some success. The economic growth of the 1990s allowed government agencies and private corporations to accommodate further cost increases. However, eventually all economic upturns end, tax receipts fall, and profits suffer. Governments look to reduce deficit spending, and employers look for ways to trim expenses. Often, the first place they look is health care, because, in the famous words of bank robber Willie Sutton, "That's where the money is."

THE DRAIN ON THE U.S. ECONOMY

To understand why payers throughout the world are so concerned about rising health care spending, we need look no further than the U.S. health economy, the world's largest. In 1960, U.S. health care spending was about $25 billion, which represented 5 percent of the gross domestic product (GDP) or less than $150 per capita. Health care was an important policy issue, but the debate back then centered on how to *expand* utilization to those who lacked insurance, not how to cut back. In 1965, Congress passed legislation to create the Medicare insurance program for the elderly and the Medicaid program for the poor. These programs contributed to a remarkable explosion in health care spending. During the period between 1967 and 1980, spending doubled, even after accounting for inflation. By 1980, health care spending accounted for 9 percent of the GDP, or $1,000 per capita.

In the 1980s, rapidly proliferating medical technologies, including CT scans, radiation therapy for cancer, artificial hips, and open heart surgery, spurred further increases in spending. By 1990, health care spending in the United States had topped $700 billion, or about 12 percent of the GDP and $2,700 per capita. New technologies continued to emerge, including MRIs and PET scanners, advanced ventilator therapies, bone marrow transplants, and drugs for treating AIDS. Under pressure to contain costs during the economic recession of the early 1990s, employers turned to managed care. This worked, at least for a while. Employer health insurance costs moderated throughout the 1990s, only to increase rapidly in the early 2000s. In the meantime, Medicare and Medicaid continued to experience double-digit annual growth. By 2002, health care spending in the United States had reached $1.4 trillion, accounting for nearly 14 percent of the GDP and $5,000 per capita.

This spending took its toll on American taxpayers, businesses, and consumers. When Medicare began in 1966, it cost about $5 billion annually, and was funded through a 1.5 percent payroll tax on the first $15,000 of income. Today, Medicare costs more than $300 billion annually, amounting to 10 percent of all federal spending. A payroll tax of 2.9 percent of all earned income funds the program. Medicare spending continues to rise, with no sign of a slowdown. The U.S. population is aging, and new technologies continually add to the cost of care. Pending legislation would require Medicare to cover prescription drugs, at an estimated additional cost of $40 billion annually. Add it all up, and this means that there will have to either be a massive infusion of new revenue for Medicare or a dramatic cutback in Medicare payments to providers.

In the same way that Medicare has become a major tax headache for the U.S. federal government, Medicaid spending is burdening state budgets. Medicaid is the largest health care program in every state, and either the largest or second largest state government program (after education). Medicaid is also the fastest growing component of nearly every state budget.

Medicaid is typically funded by state income and sales taxes. The economic boom of the 1990s boosted state coffers, allowing legislators to accommodate rapid Medicaid growth. However, the recent economic slowdown has severely pinched state budgets. States are operating with massive deficits, approaching a combined $50 billion for 2002. To cope, many states have delayed payments to providers. In Illinois, for example, some hospitals and physicians must wait three months or more for payment. This stalling tactic only delays the inevitable, however. State legislators must eventually make deep cuts in Medicaid, cut other big state programs such as education, or increase taxes. There appear to be no other solutions to balancing the budget.

Rising premium costs spell trouble for employers as well. Most employers in the United States offer health insurance to their workers and consider the premiums to be a cost of doing business, but this cost is growing out of control. Coverage for a family of four often exceeds $7,000. When combined with the Medicare payroll tax, health spending can exceed 20 percent of total employee compensation. During the 1990s, employers coped with rising premiums by encouraging employees to enroll in managed care and requiring them to contribute toward the cost of insurance. However, even managed care plans must cope with rising technology costs, and imposing cost sharing merely shifts the ever-increasing burden without relieving it.

Put all of this information together, and it is readily apparent that health care will be one of the leading issues confronting American policymakers in the years ahead. Political observers such as David Broder are already predicting that health care could be the top issue in the 2004 presidential election.[1]

Although other nations do not spend as much on health care as does the United States, they are just as concerned about rising costs. In Canada, health spending represents nearly half of some provincial budgets. The primary source of funding for the German system is a payroll tax that exceeds 15 percent of earnings. Payroll taxes to support the French national health system exceed 20 percent of earnings. The British NHS accounts for one-fourth of all government spending, or twice what the government spends on education. With its costs spiraling upward, the future of the NHS was the central issue in the 2001 British campaign for prime minister. Tony Blair promised to put more money into the NHS, and began to do so in 2002. However, with the British economy faltering, the government may be unable to follow through any further on the promise.

TARGETING TECHNOLOGY

Most health economists believe that medical technology is the number one culprit behind four decades of continuous, worldwide increases in health spending. Speaking on behalf of executives at dozens of large corporations, Midwest Business Group on Health President Jim Mortimer also pointed his finger at the rising costs of medical technology. Many employers are specifically concerned about the rising costs of prescription drugs. Prescription drugs account for more than 20 percent of total premium costs in some plans, a figure that could climb even higher.[2] Pharmacogenomics, the next big thing in the biotech revolution, promises to create drugs that are customized to each individual's unique genetic makeup. The resulting products will be absorbed faster with fewer side effects. However, development and testing will be much more complex. If we want to enjoy the benefits, we will have to pay the price.

The march of new medical technology seems unlikely to slow down any time soon. If the past is prologue, then the promise of better lives will be accompanied by a steep price tag. Many people may view this as a threat to their economic well-being. They should instead view this as an opportunity. Under normal circumstances, we welcome innovation. We enjoy the benefits of spending money on cellular phones, handheld computers, and DVD players; we should feel the same way about health care.

Health care payers don't see it this way. Encumbered by the mindset that "health care spending is inefficient," they will continue their efforts to cap total spending. However, they may soon find that the old cost containment strategies have run their course:

1. *Require patients to make higher copayments.* The RAND study suggests that copayments have diminishing returns as a cost containment tool. Small copayments have a small deterrence effect on spending, but high copayments do not have a big deterrence effect. Besides, high copayments defeat the purpose of insurance, which is to protect individuals from financial risk. The French met with stiff resistance when they tried to increase the ticket moderateur, and other payers are likely to face similar responses from their constituents.

2. *Reduce provider fees and prices for prescription drugs.* This will shift the burden to providers and drug makers. In the short run, providers will either churn patients, requiring layers of bureaucratic oversight, or

stop seeing them altogether. In the long run, the best and brightest college students will pursue other careers besides medicine, and medical technology firms will cut back on research and development investments. Does anyone really want to slow down the march of medical science?

3. *Use a budget cap to place blanket restrictions on the availability of new drugs and technologies.* We have seen the consequences of budget controls in Canada and England. Further budget tightening will only lengthen queues and increase suffering.

Payers understand that their cost containment options are limited. Some payers are jumping on the health promotion bandwagon. Changes in diet and health habits will only go so far to contain health care costs, though. Even the most virtuous among us must eventually face life-threatening illnesses and will want access to the most complete arsenal of treatments that medical science has to offer. Improved health behaviors may offer a brief and valuable respite from rising health costs. However, the days of cost containment seem to be coming to a close.

THE FALLACY OF COST CONTAINMENT

The conventional wisdom may be that we are not getting our money's worth out of our health care dollars. The conventional wisdom is wrong, debunked by cost–benefit analysis. Rising health care spending can be a good thing! Increased spending buys the most precious of commodities: longer, healthier lives.

If it made sense to limit health care spending, one would expect payers to come to some agreement on where to draw the line. The Canadians, French, and Germans once seemed content to draw the line at about 10 percent of GDP. However, the German government has allowed spending to creep up, and the Canadian government is under tremendous political pressure to do the same. Britons balked at the idea of spending 8 percent of their GDP, but now seem willing to pour more money into health care. Americans began to wring their hands about health care spending in the 1970s, when it accounted for just 8 percent of the GDP. We agonized again in the 1980s when spending rose to 10 percent, and seriously debated a government takeover of the system as the figure rose to 13 percent and threatened to grow to as much as 20 percent by 2000.

Nowadays, no one in the United States is seriously proposing that we reduce spending to 10 percent of GDP, let alone 8 percent. Our lives would be shorter and sicker. We might look back one day and wonder how we ever managed to spend as little as 13 percent of our GDP on health care. The fact is that there is no correct percentage of GDP to spend on health care. If additional health care spending buys us additional years of healthy living, then 20 percent might be justified. It might even be too little.[3]

Too many health care payers view cost containment as their ultimate objective. It is even written into the German *Konzertierte Aktion*. Payers have lost sight of their true purpose, which is to assure that health care dollars are spent wisely, regardless of the level of spending. To this end, copayments, fee ceilings, and other cost containment measures have their place. U.S. managed care organizations (MCOs) have successfully implemented all of these strategies, but even the most tightly managed HMOs are currently facing double-digit inflationary pressures.

THE STEADY DRUMBEAT OF RATIONAL RATIONING

Any effort to make sense out of health care spending must eventually come to terms with medical technology. Most payers use blunt instruments—budget controls, limits on specialty training, and referral restrictions—to hold down technology costs. None of these methods assures patients that they are getting the technologies they need, now or in the future. The time has come for payers to embrace methods that specifically weigh benefits and costs. The time has come for rational rationing.

Slowly but surely, payers are embracing rational rationing methods. England's NICE and Australia's PBAC are just the beginning. Using a system known as the "Dutch Funnel," the Netherlands government uses a series of four "sieves" to filter out those services that the government will not pay for. One of the sieves is cost-effectiveness. Many Canadian provinces use cost-effectiveness criteria to allocate their limited funds.

In the United States, CEA/CBA methods show up in the creation of prescription drug formularies and, most controversially, in the practice of utilization review (UR). Most MCOs require providers to get permission from UR agencies prior to expensive treatments. UR agencies use evidence from CEA studies to justify their decisions, but UR agencies also increase the bureaucratic obstacles to delivering care. This infuriates physicians. Seeking to avoid the hassle, many physicians hesitate before recommending costly treatments, which is apparently one of the main reasons why UR saves money.

Physicians may detest UR, but it actually evolved from the use of CEA methods by the medical community. CEA studies in medical journals help physicians identify inappropriate decisions and develop programs to correct mistakes. Many provider organizations have formalized their efforts through "disease management" programs that coordinate the entire spectrum of care, from prevention and diagnosis through treatment and recovery. The practitioners of disease management understand that CEA studies are imperfect, but imperfect studies are better than no studies. The medical community knows better than to wait for perfect data and research methods.

Physicians are no strangers to CEA methods and may fully accept rational rationing. A few years ago, the Canadian Medical Association proposed a system that resembled the Dutch funnel. The British Medical Association (BMA) recently offered its support for NICE, warts and all. The BMA acknowledged that such rationing efforts would help the NHS concentrate spending on those services that provide the greatest benefits.[4]

Payers and providers may accept rational rationing, but will patients go along? Some patients may view rational rationing as a cold-hearted effort to place dollars above lives. However, it does not have to be that way. Rational rationing can help make sure that we get the maximum possible bang for our health care bucks. All the available research suggests that new medical technologies are worth the cost. Rational rationing should confirm this. Properly performed, rational rationing should lead to higher health care spending and longer, healthier lives.

Two concerns remain. Will patients accept the rational methods of payers, and will payers respect the wishes of patients? I conclude the book by addressing these two concerns.

CAN PATIENTS BE RATIONAL?

Rational rationing would delegate life-and-death decisions to technocrats, whose number crunching will supposedly assure that we spend our health care dollars wisely. However, when it comes to spending money to save lives, we often see decisions that fly in the face of mathematical logic. These decisions make one wonder if it is possible to implement a purely rational system.

For example, consider the billions of dollars that the United States spends on programs that offer trivial health benefits. Tengs et al. identified many such programs, such as asbestos removal. Prior to his appointment to the U.S. Supreme Court, Stephen Breyer published *Breaking the Vicious Circle,* in which he criticized spending on such high-cost/low-benefit interventions.[5] He observed that the risk of dying from breathing the air in a building constructed with asbestos fire retardant is the same as the risk of dying from breathing fresh country air. Removing the asbestos is a complete waste of money. Breyer also questioned spending in excess of $100 billion to clean up toxic waste sites. He pointed out that just a tiny fraction of that money could be used to save many more lives, by assuring the vaccination of 18-month-olds against a virus that causes bacterial meningitis, or by funding routine mammograms.

So why does the United States spend billions of dollars on high-cost/low-benefit interventions, even as far more valuable interventions are wanting for funds? CEA/CBA methods may be based on scientific principles, but government spending decisions are far from scientific. Politics plays a big role, which means that policymakers must cater to concerns of interest groups and voters. Environmental interest groups have an especially influential voice in Washington, and they have successfully overstated the risks of a host of environmental hazards. At the same time, voters are not very good when it comes to assessing health risks. Breyer cited an Environmental Protection Agency (EPA) study in which the public and EPA experts ranked the health risks of various environmental problems. The public fears harm from polluted waterways, radioactive waste, and industrial accidents, but dismisses risks from indoor air pollution, indoor radon, and acid rain. EPA experts dismiss the former, but express grave concern about the latter. The public is just as poorly informed about broader classes of health risks. For example, the public greatly overestimates risks from tornadoes, cancer, botulism, and homicide, but underestimates risks from less "glamorous" causes such as stroke, asthma, and diabetes.

There are several candidate explanations for why the public does such a poor job at evaluating risk. People usually overestimate the risk of events that have been sensationalized in the media. Americans stayed away from the beaches in the late summer of 2001 due to widespread media coverage of shark attacks. Yet the frequency of shark attacks in 2001 was actually lower than average, and virtually all the attacks were confined to surfers. None of that mattered to bathers who saw pictures of the attack victims. Thanks to media coverage in the summer of 2002, parents throughout the United States worried that their children might be kidnapped. The media scarcely mentioned that child abduction rates had been steadily declining for decades. NICE experienced the power of the media in the beta interferon debacle. The media will not get involved in every rational rationing decision, but can help undermine public confidence in the process. Interest groups understand the powerful role of the media, and their efforts can help convince the public of the "importance" of relatively minor problems.

The media are not the only source of irrationality. People tend to dwell on "dreaded" adverse events such as cancer, and discount the possibility of "acceptable" adverse events, such as heart disease. We also overstate the risk of events over which we have no control, such as airplane crashes.

If the patients who must pass judgment on rational rationing are ill-informed about risk, they may be quick to criticize policies that actually save lives. The Oregon legislature rejected Robert Kaplan's rankings out of hand because they seemed counterintuitive and likely to spark protests, not because they were technically incorrect. The lobbying of AIDS activists and child-welfare organizations must have also been on the mind of Oregon legislators. If rational rationing methods spread, we can expect a lot more of the same, unless the public and the media are educated about CEA/CBA methods and political meddling is kept to a minimum.

WHO SHOULD RATION?

Rational rationing is based in scientific principles. Medical, statistical, and economic models tell researchers how to compute costs, determine the discount rate, measure health benefits, and even to put a dollar value on them. However, scientific principles do not lead all researchers to the same answers. The scientific community disagrees about many of the finer points of CEA/CBA analysis.

The result is that researchers can reach different conclusions about the cost-effectiveness of a particular treatment. Researchers may examine different populations that react differently to the treatment. Accounting standards for cost measurement are an oxymoron. There is no consensus on the appropriate discount rate. Survey methods for measuring benefits are equally inexact, and there is considerable disagreement about how to quantify benefits. Researchers may even select cost measures, discount rates, and so on, so as to tilt research findings in one direction or another.

Yet none of these concerns are enough to throw in the towel and abandon the effort. Imprecise rational rationing beats pure guesswork, provided that the payers who must read and interpret the research studies are aware of the potential biases. By all accounts, payers are prepared for the challenge. Payer technology review panels are filled with leading academic researchers at the forefront of CEA/CBA methods. Of course, some imprecision in CBA/CEA research is inevitable. More often than not, payers will see right through biased methods and identify those technologies that are likely to be cost-effective.

When Oregon wanted to develop a priority list that was free of bias, it turned to Robert Kaplan, a well-respected scholar. Kaplan produced a list that was imprecise, but probably without any systematic biases in favor of one interest group or another. Oregon rejected Kaplan's list for political expediency, yet the final list still seems to be an improvement over the status quo. After all, it is not as if the status quo was free of political biases. The same balancing of science and politics has shown up elsewhere. NICE may have waffled on Relenza and beta interferon, and Australia's PBS caved in to pressure from Pfizer to pay for Viagra, but both agencies have rejected numerous interventions of limited value, freeing up millions of dollars in the process.

RATIONAL RATIONING
IN THE PUBLIC SECTOR

It seems that government agencies are able to develop reasonable cost-effectiveness measures and keep political intrusions to a tolerable level. Two factors may help explain their success. First, they have yet to deal with many big-ticket items such as neonatology, hip replacements, and bypass surgery. These cost billions of dollars and affect hundreds of thousands of patients. When NICE and PBAC have dealt with high-profile issues such as Viagra, the political heat has been turned on full blast. Second, government agencies appear to have wisely incorporated a large gray area into their analyses. Government payers usually accept interventions that have a CEA ratio below $20,000 per QALY and reject those with a ratio above $60,000. This helps eliminate some controversy, as a supplier cannot make a strong case for approval of a drug with a CEA ratio above $60,000 when the threshold for approval is $20,000. Unfortunately, the gray area between $20,000 and $60,000 contains dozens of common medical interventions. For interventions such as cervical cancer screening, multiple-vessel bypass surgery, or renal dialysis, all of which fall in this gray area, politics will necessarily play an important role in access decisions.

The inevitable intrusion of politics in the gray area is only the beginning of the problems that emerge when government agencies attempt to rationally ration. Foot dragging can lead to intolerable delays in access: Just consider the two years it took for NICE to reach its "compromise" verdict on beta interferon. Australia's PBAC often requires a year or more to decide on drugs that have already been approved as medically safe and effective. At least PBAC has managed to review most drugs. To date, NICE has issued fewer than 50 guidances, covering just a small percentage of total health care interventions. It will take many more guidances if Great Britain is to free up the resources it needs to end postcode rationing.

To judge from the guidances issued to date, the issuance of 500 more will not resolve the final obstacle to an acceptable rational rationing plan. As far as can be told, every government body that has established a cost-effectiveness threshold, including NICE, has set the bar too low. Government payers are only willing to commit to paying for services below the $20,000 per QALY threshold. However, our lives are worth far more, upwards of $150,000 per QALY.

Any payer that goes down the path of rational rationing must decide where it will set the cost-effectiveness threshold. Thus far, politicians and medical researchers have made most of those decisions. Let the public join in the debate. I suspect that if all our voices were heard, pressure to *increase* health spending would intensify, even if it means higher taxes or cutbacks in other programs. Regulated health care systems have kept artificial ceilings on health expenditures for too long. If new technologies can substantially improve the quality and quantity of life, then let's bring them on!

There is, of course, an alternative to publicly funded health care and the need to thrash out rationing schemes and budget levels in the political arena. In the final section of this book, I examine the potential for rational rationing in the competitive U.S. health care system.

RATIONAL RATIONING AND MANAGED CARE

Through formularies and UR, MCOs have already taken the first steps toward rational rationing. They have proven to be fast, effective, and, to a certain extent, responsive to patients. Pharmacy and therapeutics committees that establish formularies keep abreast of all the pharmacoeconomic studies. These committees have been especially fast and responsive, reviewing drugs within just a few months of Food and Drug Administration (FDA) approval, and usually approving even the costliest of new drugs. UR agencies are also well versed in CEA methods. They rarely issue blanket rejections of costly treatments, although they can create some hassles for physicians and patients.

The tools are in place for MCOs to implement rational rationing, but several things are holding them back. First and foremost, most MCOs understand that further access restrictions would be the kiss of death in the marketplace. Lacking the monopoly power of government-run health care systems, MCOs must respond to the demands of the market. Americans want access to the latest technologies, and MCOs give it to them. MCOs may limit access relative to traditional indemnity insurance, but not when compared with government-run systems in other countries.

For proof that MCOs have met the needs of the market-place, one need only look at the huge market shares of HMOs and PPOs in comparison with paltry shares of traditional indemnity insurers. Indeed, one of the advantages of a competitive health care market is that individuals who place a higher value on their life are able to select health plans that afford greater access. (Remember that valuations can differ dramatically from one person to the next.) The success of HMOs and PPOs suggests that Americans are willing to tolerate some access restrictions, if handled correctly. Critics complain that the success of HMOs and PPOs merely reflects the desire of employers to cut health care costs, rather than the wishes of their employees. It might even indicate that MCOs have maintained a veil over their allegedly harmful practices. Rational rationing would simply institutionalize greed. By this logic, it is a wonder that MCOs pay for any services at all. Remember, there is no systematic evidence that the quality of care has suffered. In fact, dozens of detailed studies suggest that the quality of care received by patients in MCOs is as good, or better, than the quality of care received by patients with traditional health insurance. MCO-style rationing—a mix of incentives and UR-based utilization controls—seems to be working.

There is only one way to explain these facts: Greed might motivate some MCO executives, but market forces keep that greed in check. When MCOs cut costs, the market forces them to pass the savings along to employers in the form of lower premiums. Employers then use the cost savings in a number of ways: to boost wages, reduce prices, or increase their own profits. One way or another, the vast majority of savings from cost containment efforts ends up benefiting the public, not HMOs.

The critics are correct to a certain extent, however. MCOs must win the support of employers before they can enroll individual subscribers. If all employers share Mr. Mortimer's views about the benefits of technology, this might encourage MCOs to further restrict access. However, employers must also answer to the market. In the past five years, employers have steadily switched to more generous health care benefits, reflecting the desires of employees for the greatest possible access to services. Premiums have increased as a result. Employers have passed some of the increase on to employees. Employees have complained, but few of them are opting for less costly coverage. Less restrictive PPOs have been gaining market share at the expense of HMOs, and HMOs themselves have become less restrictive while increasing premiums. As long as employees believe it is worth the cost, health care benefits will continue to expand.

The market should also work to make rational rationing a success. MCOs would certainly be forced to go public with their CEA thresholds. Given that MCO patients in the United States have greater access to costly medical services than do patients in government-funded systems elsewhere, there is every reason to believe that MCOs would adopt CEA thresholds that exceed $20,000 to $60,000. If WTP studies are wrong, and patients really prefer lower thresholds, then the market will reward stingier MCOs. In any case, patients will get a level of rationing that they can live with.

The market should also diminish the role of politics. Multiple sclerosis sufferers may howl in protest if an MCO decides not to pay for beta interferon, but if this decision enables the MCO to offer a package of high-quality care at a reasonable cost, it will put up with the protests. MCOs will have to contend with the imprecision of CEA methods, but the market could be a powerful force for improving those methods. If the public is privy to the methods they use, then those MCOs that get it right will end up with the lion's share of enrollees.

THE REAL OBSTACLES

Despite the obvious benefits of rational rationing by MCOs, some significant obstacles remain. For now, it would not be politically expedient for MCOs to change the way they restrict access. Federal legislators are prepared to enact tough new laws that could put managed care out of business, and rational rationing is sure to invite unwanted controversy. MCOs also face the risk of potential lawsuits. They already face a major class action lawsuit alleging that they do not provide the level of care guaranteed in their policies. I cannot imagine any MCO wanting to be the first to impose new access restrictions, even if, on balance, the restrictions lead to higher levels of care. As long as some patients are adversely affected, the legal liability could be enormous.

This is not to say that a full retreat by politicians and lawyers would herald the era of rational rationing in the United States. Patients continue to be suspicious of MCOs, and would undoubtedly be skeptical of a scheme that purports to save lives yet is too technical for a layperson to fully understand. For this reason, it will be imperative for MCOs to win the support of physicians, who must be shown that rational rationing will expand access and save lives, not have the opposite effect.

Better still, MCOs could show directly that their methods are saving lives. Unfortunately, this will require data on utilization and outcomes that can be very difficult to collect. Many MCOs and providers have been attempting to assemble electronic medical records for performing this kind of quality evaluation. Unfortunately, privacy protection measures in the Health Insurance Portability and Accountability Act of 1996 (HIPAA) has seriously hindered their efforts. It would be sadly ironic if, in the name of protecting patient privacy, HIPAA prevents the adoption of MCO strategies that could save lives.

There is one final concern about rational rationing. The competitive market will encourage plans to select different levels of rationing, so as to tailor their offerings to meet the varying needs of different consumers. However, it is possible that some MCOs will use restrictive rationing as a ploy to discourage sick, high-cost patients from enrolling. Such concerns are an inevitable part of a competitive health insurance market. In recent years, large purchasing groups such as the Pacific Business Group on Health have used their market clout to assure that MCOs do not use such exclusionary tactics. Provided the balance of power between group purchasers and MCOs can be maintained, this should not be a serious obstacle to rational rationing.

RATIONAL RATIONING IN THE 21ST CENTURY

Rational rationing has already arrived. Elements of it are central to health systems in Australia, Canada, Germany, Great Britain, the Netherlands, and even the United States. Wherever it is adopted, payers can expect to face histrionics and lawsuits from some patients and providers, but patients and providers must understand that the alternatives to rational rationing are far worse.

We are at a crossroads. Payers have decided that enough is enough, and they want to hold the line on spending growth. They are doing this without a serious assessment of the benefits and costs of health care spending. Yet CEA/CBA studies show that health care is a bargain, and that we should be embracing new technologies. The time has come to put all the benefits and costs of health care on the table. I fully expect that this will convince payers of the need to spend more money on health care, not less.

ENDNOTES

1. D. Broder, 2002, "Health Care in a Death Cycle," *Washington Post*, 17 April 2002, p. A15.

2. Many drugs produce offsetting cost savings; for example, through reduced hospital use.

3. At some point, diminishing returns will set in, but it seems doubtful that we have reached the point where we are giving up too much of other goods and services to live a bit longer and a bit healthier.

4. See J. Hope, 2001, "In Need of a Hospital Bed? Try Germany," *London Daily Mail,* 7 February 2001, p. 23.

5. S. Breyer, 1993, *Breaking the Vicious Circle.* Cambridge, MA: Harvard University Press.

INDEX

A

Aaron, Henry, 128
Acetylcholinesterase inhibitors, 16
Age-adjusted value of a life-year, 149
Allegra, 75
Assurance Maladie (France), 30, 43
Australia:
    Breast Cancer Network Australia, 9
    cost-effectiveness analysis (CEA),
        and drug approval process,
        9
    costs per quality-adjusted life-years
        (QALY), 136
    government payers in, 1
    health care spending, 41
    medical technology, availability and
        use of, 42
    Pharmacy Benefits Scheme (PBS),
        8–9, 78, 83, 171
    cost-effectiveness threshold used
        by, 158
    and Viagra (Pfizer), 175
    rational rationing in, 181
    rationing in, 8–10
    value of a life, 136
    Viagra, PBAC's approval of, 9–10

B

"Bargain" interventions, 35
BBB defense, 26–27

Benefit-cost trade-offs, 164
Beta-blocker therapy, 88
Beta-interferon controversy, 4–5, 15–17,
    174
"Biggest bang for the buck" (BBB)
        rationing defense, 26–27
Blair, Tony, 13, 167
Breaking the Vicious Cycle (Breyer),
    172–73
Breyer, Stephen, 172–73
Broad health states, 99
Brown, Lawrence, 129
Budget controls, 169
Bush, George H. W., 131
Bush, George W., 135

C

Canada:
    Canada Health Act of 1984, 49
    cost-effectiveness threshold used
        by, 158
    costs per quality-adjusted life-years
        (QALY), 136
    drawing the line, 169–70
    government payers in, 1
    health care spending, 41
    health care system, 81
    origins of, 49
    medical technology, availability and
        use of, 42
    physicians, access to, 42

primary care physicians (PCPs),
access to, 50
provincial programs, differences in,
49–50
rational rationing in, 181
rationing in, 49–52
future of, 51–52
specialist referrals, 50
universal public health insurance
system, 5
value of a life, 136
waiting lists, 50–51
Cancer prevention, 92
Carte Vitale (French), 30
Categorically needy recipients of health
care services, 118
CEA, 78, See Cost-effectiveness analysis
(CEA)
Celebrex, 5, 10, 74
Certainty premium, 150
Certificate-of-need (CON) laws, 64
Chemotherapy:
cost of, 89–90
and health care payers, 88–89
Children's Defense Fund, and rationing,
6
Children's Hospital of Philadelphia,
separation of Siamese
twins, 36–37
Claritin, 75
Clinton, William (Bill) Jefferson, 129,
131
plan for universal coverage, 61–62,
135
Cohort studies, 86
Colorado, and rationing, 133
Copaxone, 73–74
Copayments, 31, 81, 164, 168
Cost-benefit analysis (CBA), 84–85
Cost containment, 3–4
fallacy of, 169–70
Cost-effectiveness analysis (CEA), 82–
96
background, 83
CBA/CEA analysis, 84–90, 171, 173
method summary, 113–14

in practice, 93–95
validity of, 92–93
cohort studies, 86
discounting, 90–91
published studies, reliability of, 86–
87
and U.S. Army Corps of Engineers,
83
U.S. government agency use of, 83
use of, 83–85
Cost of illness (COI) approach, 143–45,
156
Cost-per-lost-life, 144
Costs per quality-adjusted life-years
(QALY), 14, 16, 17, 74–75
Culyer, Anthony, 18
Cutler, David, 158–59

D

Demand inducement, 33–35, 43, 163
Diagnosis-related group (DRG), 66
Dialysis, cost-effectiveness of, 35, 37
Digital rectal exam (DRE), 97
Dillon, Andrew, 4–5
Direct COI, 144
Direct-to-consumer (DTC) advertising,
75–76
Disability-Adjusted Life-Years (DALYs),
98
Discounting, 90–91
Disease management, 70, 171
Disproportionate share hospitals, 60
Diversified Pharmacy Services, 72
Dobson, Frank, 12, 13
Dollar value of health, 141–42
Drug costs, rise in, 77
Drugmaker strategies, 74–75
DTC, See Direct-to-consumer (DTC)
advertising
Dutch Funnel, 171
DVQALY, 159

E

Effexor, 76

Ellwood, Paul, 66
England:
    drawing the line, 169–70
    government payers in, 1
    health care spending, 41
    health care system, 81
    medical technology, availability and
        use of, 42
    National Health Service (NHS), 10–
        11, 30, 52, 67
    and Relenza (Glaxo), 12
    reorganization of, 53–54
    National Institute for Clinical
        Excellence (NICE), 4–5, 8,
        10–19, 52, 78, 83, 171
    and acetylcholinesterase
        inhibitors, 16
    beta-interferon controversy,
        15–17
    British Medical Association
        (BMA) support for, 171
    cost-effectiveness threshold
        used by, 158
    costs per quality-adjusted life-
        years (QALY), 14, 16, 17
    creation of, 11
    guidances, 12–15
    medicine versus economics,
        17–19
    and Meridia, 17
    negative guidance, 17
    negative publicity received by,
        19
    and postcode rationing, 12
    and Relenza (Glaxo), 12–13,
        175
    and Ritalin, 16
    role of, 11–12
    taxanes, approval of, 13
    trade-offs between money and
        lives, 14
    and Visudyne, 17
    per capita spending on health care,
        52
    postcode lottery, 11, 52
    primary care, access to, 53

    private health insurance, purchase
        of, 54
    rational rationing in, 181
    rationing in, 52–54
    value of a life, 136
    waiting lists, 52–54
Enthoven, Alain, 66
Environmental Protection Agency
    (EPA), 145, 173
European Quality of Life (EuroQoL)
    scale, 110–11
Evans, Robert, 34, 43
Express Scripts, 72

F

Fabian, Robert, 145, 147–48, 150
"Five-Hundred Life-Saving
    Interventions and Their
    Cost-Effectiveness," 35
Flexner Commission, 68
Food and Drug Administration (FDA),
    173
"Formularies," 7
Formularies, 73–75
Foxe, Fanny, 62
Framing problem, 150
France:
    Assurance Maladie, 30, 43
    copayment (ticket moderateur), 31,
        55, 81
    drawing the line, 169–70
    health care spending, 41
    health care system, 30
    medical technology, availability and
        use of, 42
    rationing in, 54–55
    vacation packages to hospitals, 54
Fuchs, Victor, 34

G

Genentech, 93–95
Germany:
    churning, 45–46, 48
    Cost-Containment Act of 1977, 44

discounted hospital stays, offer of, 54
division between hospital-based physicians and other physicians, 46
drawing the line, 169–70
drug costs, controlling, 46–48
government payers in, 1
health care costs, rise in, 48
health care spending, 41
health care system, 44
Konzertierte Aktion, 44, 46, 48, 170
medical technology, availability and use of, 42
national health system, 30
Neuordnungsgesetze (NOG), 46–48
physician expenditures, cap on, 45–46
physicians, access to, 42
rational rationing in, 181
rationing in, 44–48
sickness funds, 30, 44–46
uniform pricing, 44–45
Glaxo, 12
Global Utilization of Streptokinase and Tissue Plasminogen Activator for Occluded Coronary Arteries trial, 94–95
Gore, Al, 118, 125, 129
Government payers, xiii, 1
Government-sponsored rationing, 64–66
Great Britain, *See* England:
Grossman, Michael, 140–41
Group Health Cooperative (GHC) of Puget Sound, 34, 66, 67
GUSTO, 94–95

H

Health care, *See also* U.S. health care system; specific countries
and societal resources, 2–3
Health Care Finance Administration (HFCA), 131–32
Health care payers:

and cap on total spending, 168–69
and CBA/CEA analysis, 91–92
and chemotherapy, 88–89
claim of inefficient health care spending, 163–64
and clinical evidence, 12
and cost containment, 4, 7–8, 18, 164–65, 169–70
drawing the line, xiv, 77–78, 169
and drug costs, 77
government payers, xiii, 1, 176
and health care spending, 165
moral hazard theory, 35
and new technologies, 3
and published studies, 93
and rational rationing, xiv
and rationing, 2
rationing, defense of, 38–39
and system inefficiencies, 81, 83
and technology costs, 170–71
and value of life, 136, 156
and WOM defense, 27
Health care spending, 3–4, 77–78
international comparison of, 41
rise in, 77, 164–67
U.S. economy, drain on, 165–67
Health insurance:
Americans without, 60–61
costs, rise in, xiii
and rationing by price, 4
Health Insurance Portability and Accountability Act of 1996 (HIPAA), 180
Health maintenance organizations (HMOs), 64, 66–67
and DTC ads, 76
"formularies," 7
and Oregon health plan, 123–24
origin of term, 66
physician bonuses for cost containment, 3
rationing, 18–19
of prescription drugs, 7
Health states, 98–102
broad, 99
examples of, 99

narrow, 99
Healthy Year Equivalents (HYEs), 98
Henry V (King of England), 151–52
Herceptin (Roche), 9
HMOs, See Health maintenance
  organizations (HMOs)
Hospital prices, regulation of, 64
Hospital quality committees, 68
Human capital, use of term, 141
Human capital value of health, 141

I

Identified lives, defined, 151
Indemnity insurance, institutional
  barriers faced by patients
  with, 63
Indirect COI, 144
Indirect costs, 88
Inducement theory, 33–35, 43
Informed judgment, 131
Institutional rationing, 19
Institutionalized rationing, 5–6
International comparison of health care
  spending, 41
Intrinsic value of health, 141
Irwin, Craig, 125

J

Japan:
  national health system, 30
  rationing in, 55
Job risk, trade-offs between money and,
  153–54
Joint Economic Committee (JEC), 143–
  44

K

Kaiser Permanente, 34, 66, 74–75
  "reversal of economics", 82
Kaplan, Robert, 110, 124–25, 127–31,
  135, 174, 175
Keegan, John, 153

Kennedy-Mills national health insurance
  proposal, 31–32, 61–62
Kennedy, Ted, 31–32, 61
Kitzhaber, John, 6, 118, 121–24, 130–
  33, 151
Klevit, Harvey, 126
Koppel, Ted, 122

L

Lamm, Richard, 126
League tables, 101
Life, placing a dollar value on, 1–3
Lipitor, 75
Low-dose aspirin therapy, cost per year
  of life save, 155
"Low-hanging fruit," 134
Luft, Harold, 66

M

Mammograms, 92
Managed care organizations (MCOs), 3,
  65, 170
  brief history of, 66–67
  and drug costs, 74
  formularies, 72–75
  patient suspicion of, 180
  pharmacy benefits management
    firms (PBMs), 72
  and rational rationing, 177–79
  and rationing, 62
  strategies for containing costs, 67–
    76
    direct-to-consumer (DTC)
      advertising, 75–76
    formularies, 73–75
    selective contracting, 72
    utilization review (UR), 68–72
  and U.S. health care spending, 67
Market-based rationing, 60–61
McCall, Nelda, 31–32
McClellan, Mark, 158–59
McKillop, Tom, 13
McNeil, Barbara, 86–87
McNerney, Walter, 66

MCOs, *See* Managed care organizations (MCOs):
Medco, 72
Medicaid:
    cost growth, 118–19
    federal government funding of, 118–19
    funding by state income/sales taxes, 166
    Health Care Finance Administration (HFCA), 131–32
    inception of program, 118
Medical decision-making authority, delegation of, 63
Medical errors, 63
Medicare/Medicaid, 165–66
    spending growth, cap on, xiii
    and unemployed Americans, 59
Mills, Wilbur, 31–32, 61–62
Money, trade-offs between risk and, 153–54
Moral hazard theory, 29–32, 163
    and excessive expenditures, 30–31
    and ubiquity of health insurance, 29–30
Mortimer, Jim, 77–78, 158–59, 168
Multiple sclerosis (MS) patients:
    beta-interferon controversy, 4–5, 15–17
    symptoms suffered by, 15

and acetylcholinesterase inhibitors, 16
beta-interferon controversy, 15–17
British Medical Association (BMA) support for, 171
costs per quality-adjusted life-years (QALY), 14, 16, 17
creation of, 11
guidances, 12–15
    negative, 17
medicine versus economics, 17–19
and Meridia, 17
negative publicity received by, 19
and postcode rationing, 12
and Relenza (Glaxo), 12–13, 175
and Ritalin, 16
role of, 11–12
taxanes, approval of, 13
trade-offs between money and lives, 14
and Visudyne, 17
Netherlands:
    Dutch Funnel, 171
    rational rationing in, 181
Nixon, Richard M., 66
Noneconomic component, September 11 compensation package, 141
Nonsteroidal anti-inflammatory drug (NSAID), 19

N

Narrow health states, 99
National drug boards, 72
National health care system, 129
National health insurance, 61–62
    cost of, 62
National Health Service (NHS), 10–11, 30, 52, 167
    and Relenza (Glaxo), 12
    reorganization of, 53–54
National Institute for Clinical Excellence (NICE), 4–5, 8, 10–19, 52, 78, 83, 171

O

Oregon health plan, 117–36
    creation of, 122–23
    drawing the line, 135–36
    Health Services Commission, 124–27, 133–34
    and HMOs, 123–24
    Medicaid patient stories, 120–21
    Medicaid program, 8, 78, 102, 118, 119
    transplant coverage, 119–20
    Oregon Health Decisions, 120
    over time, 132–35

prioritized list of health services, 124–27
revised list, 126–28
Quality of Well-Being (QWB) scale, 124–26
rationing, 6–7, 117–20, 122–31
plan performance, 131–33
protests, 128–31, 174

P

Pacific Business Group on Health, 180
Paternalism, BBB and WOM rationing and, 27
Patient outcome research teams (PORTs), 70
Paxil, 76
Peer review, 68
Pharmacogenomics, 168
Pharmacy Benefits Advisory Committee (PBAC), 5
Pharmacy benefits management firms (PBMs), 72, 76
decision-making, 74
Pharmacy Benefits Scheme (PBS), 8–9, 78, 83
Physican incentives, changing, 82
Physician discretion, 63
Physician gatekeepers, 63
Pizza analogy, 23–24
Postcode lottery, 11, 52
Practice variations, 163
Preferred provider organizations (PPOs), 67
Premium costs, rise in, 166–67
Prescription drugs, cost of, 168–69
Prevacid, 76
Price rationing, 4, 24
Prilosec, 76
Private goods, 83–84
Professional control, 68
Professional review organizations (PROs), 69–70
Professional standards review organizations (PSROs), 69
Proscar, 74

Prospective payment system (PPS), diagnosis-related group (DRG), 66
Prostate-specific antigen (PSA) test, 97–98, 114–15
Provider costs, measuring, 87–88
Provider fees, 168–69
Prozac, 76
Public goods, 83

Q

Quality-Adjusted Life-Years (QALYs), 98–99, 163
"all QALYs are equal" (AQAE) assumption, 102–3
concerns about, 111
and discrimination, 112
DVQALY, 159
equal treatment of, 102–3
league tables, 101
measuring, 103–7
relative scale approach, 104–5, 108
standard gamble approach, 105–6, 108–9
time trade-off approach, 106–7, 109–10
putting into practice, 102–10
QALY expectancy, 159
QALY scores, 99
QALY surveys, limitations of, 112–13
working with, 99–102
Quality of life, measuring, 97–115
Quality of Well-Being (QWB) scale, 110–11, 124

R

RAND National Health Insurance Experiment, 32–33, 62, 67
Randomized double-blind studies, 85–86
Rating scales, 98

measuring health states using, 98–102

Rational rationing, xiii–xiv, 170–72
  in the 21st century, 181
  basis of, 174
  defined, 4
  and managed care organizations (MCOs), 177–79
  obstacles to, 179–80
  and physicians, 171
  in the public sector, 175–77
  and rising costs, 163–65
  risk evaluation by the public, 173–74
  through cost-effectiveness analysis (CEA), 82–96

Rationing, xiii, *See also* Rational rationing
  ad hoc, xiii
  among insured Americans, 62–76
  "biggest bang for the buck" (BBB) rationing defense, 26–27
  in Canada, 5, 49–52
  defending in principle, 23–39
  in England, 52–54
  in France, 54–55
  in Germany, 44–48
  in Japan, 55
  justifying, 28
  long history of, 18–19
  by price, 4, 24
  rational, xiii–xiv
  in Scandinavia, 55
  and supporters of nationalized health systems, 42–43
  and toy shopping, 25–27
  of the uninsured, 60–61
  in the U.S., 7, 55, 59–79
  "waste of money" (WOM) rationing defense, 26–27
  widespread use of, 23–24
  worldwide, 41–55

Rawlins, Michael, 16
Reference pricing, 72
Relenza (Glaxo), 12–13
Rescue principle, 36

Research, 81–96
  measuring costs, 87–90
  published studies, reliability of, 86–87
Research designs, limitations of, 86
Richardson, Elizabeth, 159
Rising costs, and rational rationing, 163–65
Risk, trade-offs between money and, 153–54
Ritalin, 16
Rosen, Sherwin, 154

S

Scandinavia, rationing in, 55
Scitovsky, Anne, 31
Secure Horizons, 74
Selective contracting, 72
September 11 compensation package, 139
  noneconomic component, 141
Sickness funds, 30, 44–46
Smoking cessation programs, 88
Statistical lives:
  defined, 151
  estimating the value of, 154
Sykes, Richard, 13

T

Technology, 167–69
Technology costs, rise in, 77
Tengs, Tammy, 35–36, 163, 172
Thaler, Richard, 154
Third-party utilization reviews, 69–70
Tissue plasminogen activator (tPA), 93–95
Tolcapone, 5
Tolley, George, 145, 147–48, 150
Torrance, George, 98

U

Uninsured Americans, 60–61

United Healthcare, and utilization review (UR), 72
United Kingdom, *See* England:
United States, *See also* U.S. health care system:
    health care spending, 41
    rationing in, 55
Universal coverage, attempts to provide, 61–62
U.S. health care system, 28–38
    bad buys in, 35–37
    demand inducement, 33–35
    gaps in coverage, 30
    high administrative expenditures, 28–29
    interventions, 35–37
    Kennedy-Mills national health insurance proposal, 31–32
    large government programs, scaling back of, 36–37
    medical specialists, access to, 42
    medical technology, availability and use of, 42
    Medicare/Medicaid, 30, 59, 64–65
    access problems, 64
    history of, 64–65
    middle-of-the-road intervention value, 35–36
    moral hazard theory, 29–32
    physicians, access to, 42
    prospective payment system (PPS), 66
    rationing, defending, 38–39
    rationing in, 59–79
    government-sponsored rationing, 64–66
    through the marketing mechanism, 60–61
    wasteful spending, 43
    Wennberg variations, 37–38
U.S. National Cancer Institute, screening recommendations, 92
Utilization review (UR), 68–72, 171
    goal of UR service agencies, 70
    and MCOs, 72
    and physicians, 171
    profit motive, 71–72
    worthiness of, 71

V

Value of a life, 139–60
    cost containment, fallacy of, 169–70
    cost of illness (COI) approach, 143–45, 156
    determining, 139–40
    dollar value of health, 141–42
    economic approach to determining, 151–55
    human capital value of health, 141, 156–57
    intrinsic value of health, 141
    pricing in the real world, 142–43
    statistical vs. identified lives, 150
    surveys, using to determine, 145–49
    technology, 167–69
    U.S. government's view of, 139–40
    value of a QALY, 157–58
    willingness to pay (WTP), 140–41
Value of life, and health care payers, 136, 156
Value Rx, 72
Ventilator therapy, 92
Viagra (Pfizer), 9, 11, 74, 175
    and DTC ads, 75
Viscusi, W. Kip, 154–55, 157
Visudyne, 17

W

Waiting lists, 50–54, 82
Waits for patients, 5
"Waste of money" (WOM) rationing defense, 26–27
Wennberg, Jack, 37
Who Shall Live? (Fuchs), 2–3
Willingness to pay (WTP), 140–41, 152, 156–57
WOM defense, 26–27
Wooldridge, Michael, 10

Z

Zocor, 75
Zoloft, 76